GET THE

DUCK

OUT OF MY

POND

HOW TO START A BUSINESS WITH YOUR TEEN, BUILD THEIR CONFIDENCE & LAUNCH THEM SUCCESSFULLY INTO ADULTHOOD

SANDY BRANTLEY

AUTHOR ACADEMY elite

Library of Congress Cataloging-in-Publication Data is available upon request.

Paperback: ISBN 978-1-64085-644-8
Hardback: ISBN 978-1-64085-645-5
Ebook: ISBN 978-1-64085-646-2

Also Available in hardcover, softcover, e-book, and audiobook.

Cover Design Zeljka Kojic
Author Photo Credit Sean Brantley

CONTENTS

PART 1: DEFINING THE PROBLEM

1. Help! The Duck is Drowning 3
2. The Sitting Duck 15
3. The Secret Weapon 29

PART 2: CREATING THE PLAN

4. Playing in the Same Pond 39
5. The Flight Plan 89

PART 3: APPLYING THE PROCESS

6. Rewarding Them Right 121
7. A Matter of Character 127
8. Make a Difference 157

Acknowledgments 162
Recommended Resources 164
About the Author 167

PART 1

DEFINING THE PROBLEM

CHAPTER 1
HELP! THE DUCK IS DROWNING

When the phone rang, I knew exactly who it was. If I'm honest, I was sort of annoyed. I was busy and didn't have time for nonsense that day. There was always one thing that could interrupt my schedule in a hiccup: that ominous call every mom knows is about to change the course of her day. I know because it was happening almost everyday. I would pick up the phone to a *sick* child on the other end, wanting to come home from school. It was becoming more and more frustrating. I would pick her up, and these phantom tummy aches would miraculously get better the moment we entered the door to our house, even sooner if we passed her favorite fast food restaurant on the way. At first, I thought Samantha simply needed to toughen up a little— after all, a little tummy ache was not reason enough to come home. Clearly, they weren't real stomach pains anyway. She was probably bored at school, or maybe she wasn't getting along with one of her classmates—so I thought.

Samantha was tender-hearted and shy. A people pleaser, she didn't understand why anyone would be mean towards others. She allowed other kids to take advantage of her kind nature. Being nice didn't seem to make things any easier for her at school. As a heavy girl, she was unfortunately an easy target for teasing. If someone at school was teasing her, she needed to grow some thicker skin, right? Who hadn't dealt with a mean girl at some point growing up? We all have and we survived. Why should she be any different?

When the call came each day, I would fuss at her and tell her to stick it out. Truth be told, most days I would tell her to "suck it up." I assured her I would be there to pick her up as soon as school was over. Day after day, the calls were the same. Day after day, I'd tell her the same thing...until *today*.

When I answered the call, the sound in her voice was new to me. This call was different than the rest. I had never heard her so scared.

There was a terror in her voice that immediately sent a shudder down my spine. Samantha had locked herself in a bathroom stall and called me from her cell phone, begging for help. She was terrified and uncontrollably sobbing. I dropped everything in an instant. I could not get to the school fast enough. That afternoon, I found out that my daughter had been the victim of cruel bullying. This was not the kind of bullying I nor anyone I knew had faced as a child, but cruel torment. For months, her bullies had been tormenting and threatening her in the classroom, in the hallways, after school, and even online. It had been escalating over time. Today, they had terrorized her so badly that she was afraid they were going to seriously hurt her.

Why didn't she tell me sooner? Why didn't I see it? What kind of mother doesn't know what's happening in her child's life? I had watched her shutting down. I knew she was extremely shy and had no sense of self-confidence or self-worth. She had no friends to speak of and spent all her time in her room. How did I miss those signals?

The days following that call were tough for all of us. As a family, we were angry. As her mom, I was pissed off! I had such a heavy sense of guilt. I pulled her close and cried for a few days. Secretly, I wanted to send a hit squad to take her tormentors out. That's the truth. Publicly, I was calm and focused on helping Samantha move past it.

We went to the school and spoke with the principal, teachers, and other students. The shocking part was the students all knew what had been happening. Many had watched but had been too afraid to step in. Each child had been afraid that the bullies would turn their attention to them. What was far more shocking was that the teachers, staff, and principal claimed to be unaware that anything was taking place. Their response to *fixing* the problem was less than acceptable. They told us there was nothing they could do "unless a teacher witnessed it" on property. If they witnessed the bullying, they had a no tolerance policy and would suspend the bullies. What bully is going to do anything in the presence of a teacher? Seriously? That's the best you can do? If, on the outside chance, a teacher witnessed something the best you could do is suspend? Suspend these thugs that had altered my child's emotional and physical safety? Suspend these bullies for torturing and tormenting a girl who already struggled with self-image? Suspension would not be nearly enough, and certainly doing nothing (since it had not been witnessed by an adult) was worse.

We quickly realized we needed to move her to a new school to give her a fresh start. For her personal safety and emotional security, we had to take her out of that toxic environment. We had no recourse on the kids involved, but we could protect Samantha and begin the process of healing. We also locked down her access to social media. She did not need to see or hear what any of them were saying. We removed her from every situation where these bullies could gain access to her. Removing her from the active bullying was only the first step to true healing.

Eventually, the real question started to bubble to the surface. What do we do now? How do we rebuild her self-confidence? High school would be over in a few years, and she needed to be ready to handle college and adulthood. I had no idea where to go or what to do. We talked to school administrators, guidance counselors, psychologists, other parents, and even our pastor. None of them had a solution. Bullying does such damage to a child, yet no one knew what to do to make it better. What's worse is no one wanted to offer solutions, seemingly for fear of their ideas failing. So we were on our own. If we hoped to make a difference in Samantha's future, we had to come up with our own solution. Little did we know that our answer was coming in the most unlikely way.

Out of the blue, Samantha asked me to join a direct sales company with her. She had been looking for a part-time job for a while. She was hoping to put some extra money away for college. A dual-enrolled student in high school and college at the time, her class schedule made it very hard to find a job that would fit. She started researching potential jobs online and found this one. This particular company allowed teens to join the company as long as they were part of a mother/daughter team. So here she was asking me if I would do it with her. Ummmm.... No. I was not a sales person. I had no interest in being in direct sales. I lived in the corporate world. In fact, all my life I had looked down at the many stay-at-home-moms I knew who were part of direct sales. I figured they didn't have anything better to do with their time; clearly, these women were simply bored and needed something to do to keep them busy. I was about to get schooled.

I hated the idea, but I didn't want to let my daughter down. I began researching this company to find out as much as I could. Surely, there was a reason not to do this. Online research turned up nothing but positives, but still, I was skeptical. Then, we found out that the national convention was less than one week away on the other side of the country. If we could even get a ticket to go, how on earth could we find airfare and a hotel, let alone afford it? Truly nothing but divine intervention cleared the path for us to attend. My husband had frequent flyer miles for both my daughter and me to use. There happened to be one room still left at convention price at the host hotel. We found someone planning to go who was late in her pregnancy and was told she was unable to fly. She sold us her ticket. These things and a million other little things that had to fall into place suddenly did. In a day and a half, all our obstacles cleared and our trip suddenly materialized. Does anything like this ever happen? It certainly hadn't happened in my life, and I knew it wasn't happening without God's intervention. I started thinking something big was about to happen, but I didn't want to believe it.

My plan was to spend the days at the convention scrutinizing everything. If there were holes to poke in this business, I would find them. I watched the stage presentations, the class facilitators, and the other representatives. I even watched the staff behind the scenes. I was determined to find some reason not to do this. All I found was kindness, caring, and positivity. Darnit. The entire weekend we talked about the business. Samantha continued to beg. The true miracle was watching her interact and thrive with all the other women there. She was having conversations with strangers, naturally and confidently. This bullied child, who often was afraid to talk to people she had known for years, was having conversations with strangers. I was shocked, and I watched as she interacted with these women. She laughed and cried. It had been a long while since I'd seen her really laugh like that. This mother's heart was *full*.

Something happened on our flight home that made the decision to give this a try very easy for me. With a little catch in her voice, Samantha leaned over to me and said, "Mom, my whole life people have told me I am not pretty enough, skinny enough, or good enough. I watched these women this week and realized they are just like me. They are all different and beautiful. I know now that I *am* good enough the way I am... the way God made me. They are making a difference in the lives of others, and I can do the same."

"My whole life people have told me I am not pretty enough, skinny enough, or good enough. I watched these women this week and realized they are just like me. They are all different and beautiful. I know now that I *am* good enough the way I am... the way God made me. They are making a difference in the lives of others, and I can do the same."

My heart burst, and in true mom fashion, I did exactly what every mom would do: I bawled my eyes out! I mean I was in a full-out ugly cry, sitting on the airplane as people stared at me. My daughter was right. That realization, that moment was priceless. She could make a difference, and I had to give her that opportunity. I decided if we never made a dollar in this business, that moment of realization for her was worth it all. And our journey began.

To be honest, I didn't expect much from our brand-new little business. Not only did I expect Samantha to lose interest quickly, I believed our friends and family would be the only people interested in buying from her. I figured we would exhaust them in about three months and I'd be off the hook, six months on the outside. At least I would have supported her interests and gotten her out of the house a few times. Then, we could close up business, and life would go back to normal. That's winning, right? You bet. I had no idea what was about to happen.

First, I realized I owed a big apology to all the homemakers I labeled as *bored* for being in direct sales. Boy, was I wrong. The first few months were not a cakewalk. This business was a great opportunity. We needed to figure out how to use it, but had no idea how to work together. Like every parent and teen out there, we struggled to communicate and find common ground.

I realized this was a real opportunity to teach my daughter, not only about sales and business, but about life. I had to approach this business as a mentor, not as her mom. After some struggles and a few short months, we began finding real success. Within six months, we had earned our first incentive trip. Within eight months, we had a growing team across the United States and Canada. By our second national convention, Samantha was standing on the stage, accepting an award given to only one teen each year for being the most inspiring. In the words of the company's founder, Samantha was "exceptional," and we were one of the top producing mother/ daughter teams in the company.

With each success, Samantha grew and matured a little more. She was learning about money, how to talk to people, how to run a business, and even how to lead others. The more she did, the more I watched her confidence grow. Women seemed to really connect with her story. How many women haven't dealt with a mean girl or bully in their lifetime? Inherently, these women connected with Samantha on a very personal level. Samantha started every event and party by telling her very personal story. Each time, she would win over a new crowd of people, all willing to support her and her goals. That's who we are as people—we root for the underdog. We want to see a childhood success story, and Samantha was living it. With each tiny success, I watched the emotional scars from being bullied fade a little more.

Getting to this point wasn't magic—and it wasn't easy. But after months of dedicated work and encouraging each other, we operated this business together and found true triumphs. The real success would come after a few years and much more experience when she became an adult. That shy, terrified teen with zero self-confidence is now a confident, radiant young woman, thanks to the opportunity and experience of running a successful, fulfilling business with an intentional growth plan.

While I will always recommend and be grateful to the direct sales company we chose for giving us the unique opportunity to work together, it wasn't the specific company that developed the changes in Samantha. Any business your teen is capable of running can provide the opportunities for personal growth. You can choose the business that best suits your personality, interests, time availability, and financial investment. We loved that our company celebrated teens and offered regular incentives that made it fun and motivating to keep reaching new goals. If your business doesn't offer these things for you, you will need to recreate these dynamics within your business yourself to keep your teen's interest and give you goals to strive for together. You will want to consider this when choosing a business.

The key to success is to use a common goal and a strategic, intentional growth plan to develop your child's confidence and skill set. You can't tell a child to be confident. It's like telling an orange to be purple. You have to give your teen continual, repeatable opportunities that will promote confidence and growth with each positive experience. In this book, I will share with you the key things we learned throughout our journey. You will also discover how to develop your own growth plan so you can enjoy a closer relationship with your teen through creating a true partnership. Through business, any parent or caring adult can better their future generation for life after high school. By embracing strategic business practices and taking advantage of the opportunities that come from running that business with your teen *now*, your little duckling can be ready to leave the pond—and thrive—when the time comes.

CHAPTER 2
THE SITTING DUCK

Society is facing a huge epidemic today. In layman's terms it's called *Failure to Launch* Syndrome. That's a real thing—not only a movie title! Who knew? More and more adult children are struggling to leave home and live independently. They are often not able to obtain or hold down jobs, lack ambition, and struggle to build and grow substantial relationships. Comfortable at home and protected by parents who mean well but are contributing to this dangerous scenario, these adult children lack the critical ambition and know how to do better, to be better. In fact, a recent Pew study shows that for the first time in the modern era, a higher percentage of young adults ages 18 to 34 are living with their parents than those who aren't. Why?

What is Failure to Launch Syndrome? Jon Dabach with the Optimum Performance Institute says, "The transition from high school graduate to working college students and, ultimately, college graduate can be traumatic for those who lack certain life skills, resiliency, psychological health, and the support necessary for launching themselves into a life they love and embrace." Those who don't make this transition are more likely to become, what I call, "sitting ducks." Of course, we love our kids—but they need to get out of our pond and off the payroll at some point! So what do we do?

I will let sociology and psychology experts debate on the best plan of action to take when adult children have failure to launch syndrome. But, given my personal experience and the stories of other teens that run businesses, I believe we can give our kids the best chance to avoid this condition by laying the groundwork of personal and professional success long before they are ready to graduate from high school.

According to *Psychology Today*, "the young adult must have an inner motivation in order for success to be possible, and they often need guidance to gain clarity and focus in this area." There are many theories on why today's young adults aren't developing needed skills and traits. One prevailing thought (and the one I choose to adopt) is that we adults have failed to teach our kids to do for themselves.

I know, I know. You're probably thinking "Nope, not me! I don't do too much for my kids." I'm not attacking anyone's parenting skills, by any means. How you parent your children is not my business. I admit that I am guilty of doing things for my kids that they could and should have done for themselves. I "helped" my kids do school projects and homework all the time. You know what I mean? My child would tell me at dinnertime about a project they forgot was due the next day. I would drop everything, run to the store, tuck my kids into bed and go to work. In the morning I showed them their awesome completed project. I even ecstatically blurted out, "You did such a good job, honey!"

I wasn't a helicopter mom. Oh no. I'm guilty of so much worse. I was lawnmower mom. I ran right over my kids to plow the way and make everything easier for them. To make matters worse, when my son or daughter got an A on the project I completed for them, I praised them again! The truth is, Mom earned the A, yet I – and perhaps you- praised my child for effort they never put forth. And throughout this scenario, what did my child learn? She learned that mom would do her work for her. He learned that he didn't have to work hard to get a reward. In a world where every kid gets a trophy, sometimes parents focus too closely on praise and don't pay enough attention on the process to find success.

I allowed my kids to not have to think about anything. I took the responsibility to keep their schedules, ensured they were on time, met every deadline, and made it to every required activity with absolutely anything and everything they needed for it. I ran myself ragged as they coasted through childhood. They were happy. We were all happy. That's how it's supposed to be, right? Wrong. It's the struggles and the lessons learned through failure and hard work that teach kids the skills they need to succeed in life.

When we take failures, upsets and consequences of missed deadlines from them, we rob them of those critical life lessons, stunting their ability to launch successfully. I suspect many of you have done or continue to do the same things for your child as I did. But the reality is, by doing this we also rob our teens of the joy and satisfaction of a job well done. We keep them from finding the sense of self-worth and self-sufficiency they need to make the transition into adulthood. More importantly, we prevent them from learning to plan and manage their responsibilities around school, sports, activities, friends and family demands. By doing it all for them, we diminish our child's opportunity to use creativity, learn time management and so many other things. Above all else, doing everything for your teen deprives them of the self-confidence that they can succeed without your help. No parent intends to make their child feel incapable, but that's exactly what we do when we make, plan, organize, do and manage everything in their lives instead of helping them learn to do it all for themselves.

What about school? Aren't our teachers preparing our kids? Honestly, no they aren't. Our educators already have a full plate teaching the curriculum and keeping the peace in the classroom. Their job is to develop kids' academic prowess, not life skills. Their job has become increasingly difficult dealing with the tough societal problems they face on a daily basis with learning disabilities, school violence, troubled children and the challenging family dynamics of their students. That means it's up to us as parents to take back

the job that was rightfully ours to begin with…
to prepare our child to handle being an adult.

"It is NOT what you **DO** for your children, but what
you **TEACH THEM TO DO** for themselves that will
make them successful human beings."

—Ann Landers

Ann Landers could not have said it better when
she said "It is not what you do for your children,
but what you teach them to do for themselves
that will make them successful human beings."
We need to stop doing it for our kids and start
teaching them to do it for themselves. It's like
the old Chinese proverb you've likely heard
before: "Give a man a fish and he eats for a
day. Teach a man to fish and you feed him for a
lifetime." We are giving our children a fish, when
we ought to be teaching them how to fish. The
instant gratification of a good grade, perfect
attendance or a blue ribbon will not give your
child what they need to grow. It will only give
them a smile in the moment—and a possible
lifetime of struggling.

There is hope. It is never too late. You can make
a difference for your children. You need to be
intentional about teaching your offspring what

they need to know to be a thriving adult - and we need to start doing it at as young an age as possible. To do this right, you need a plan and the necessary tools to put your plan into action. In the chapters to come, I will share some tools to help you put that plan together for your family and your child's unique needs. By using standard business tactics to teach my child confidence and life skills, I created an intentional growth strategy to grow Samantha's abilities, maturity and self-confidence. I call it "The Flight Plan." In the process, we strengthened our relationship and earned some money too.

It's up to us as

PARENTS

to

take *Back*

the job that was
rightfully ours
to begin with

Starting a business together doesn't mean you'll instantly have this amazing relationship with your teen. It's also not a magic wand to grow your child's self-confidence overnight. Your business won't wondrously turn you into a millionaire and you won't necessarily live happily ever after. It will take work from both of you—no more doing the work yourself while your child sits back and reaps the benefits. You both need to be dedicated to the process and you both need to be committed to making the business work.

Notice the key word: *BOTH*. The business Samantha chose for us was a social selling (aka direct sales,) home party company. A few months into our business, we both had a rude awakening. We had an in home party with a very sweet hostess. The party started like any other one: we carried our displays and products into our host's home and set them up. A few dozen people showed up to socialize and shop. We started the party with Samantha telling her story. She told about being bullied, why she started this business and how it is making a difference for her. Customers were shocked to hear that this young teen owned a business and had tangible goals and aspirations. After her intro, I quickly began helping each customer choose his or her items. I tallied up their products, wrote out their invoices, put their stuff in a cute little container and... I looked over and saw Samantha sitting in the corner reading a book. Huh? Are you kidding me? I am in this business for *her* and she's relaxing with a book while I do all the work? Oh, no she's not!

I'd like to say I floated over to her and in my best Mary Poppins voice said something like, "Samantha, darling, can you get up and help our customers with their orders, please? Thank you, dear!" Unfortunately that's not quite what happened. I hurried over in a huff, leaned down really close to her ear and said in my best muffled-yet-threatening mom voice, "Get your butt up and go do something right now!" The words that came out of her mouth at that moment changed the course of our relationship and our business. "I don't know what to do!" she said, looking up at me from her novel. I stepped back and took a deep breath. All I could think in that moment was, "What do you mean you don't know what to do? How is that possible?" Only, she really didn't.

Samantha had helped carry everything in, set up, said hello to everyone and started the party telling her story. She had done everything I had asked of her. After that she truly didn't know what to do. She didn't have the life experiences like I had to know instinctively what needed to be done.

Her words rang in my ears for days. Of course, she didn't know what to do! I had always done it for her or told her exactly what needed to be done. I had not given her the skills to figure it out for herself, nor had I instructed her what steps to take. I was ready to change that.

It took some time, but I came up with a strategy to teach her everything she needed to know—not only for running a successful business, but to help her be successful in life. I needed to develop the entire person not simply a business owner. I had to be intentional about teaching her--without making it seem like I was. I needed to make it interesting and worth her time. I needed to show her that I valued her and her opinions. We had started this business together, now it was up to me to create a strategic training plan to keep us in the business--together. This plan would have to be adjustable. I would have to pay attention to the signals she was giving me and alter the plan as we went along. But, first I needed to lay a foundation.

Let's start at the beginning and lay the foundation of teaching your child life skills through business. Before you can begin your duckling's Flight Plan, we need to talk mindset and how changing your thinking a little bit will make all the difference as you move forward in a business with your teen.

GROWTH
doesn't happen
by *Accident*

Every kid is one **CARING** adult away from from being a *Success*

-Josh Shipp

CHAPTER 3
THE SECRET WEAPON

If you have a teen and are not including them in your business, you are leaving huge opportunity on the table. No one can say "no" to a teen trying to better his or her self. As a society we all love an underdog. We can't help but root for them to overcome the odds and win. There is no bigger underdog than a teen. We all remember how hard those days of trying to figure out where we belonged or who and what we wanted to be. Growing up is hard. If you leverage this fact to your advantage, your business can grow in ways you never thought possible.

I have two words to prove the power children can have to the bottom line, *Girl Scouts*. I am the biggest sucker for these adorable little ladies selling their cookies. Who can say "no" to them? Their cookies are good, but we don't buy their cookies for the taste and certainly not for the price. Any grocery store sells less expensive cookies that taste good. We buy them because we want to support a young lady trying to reach a goal. I would argue that these cookies would not be so popular if middle-aged women or men sold them for profit. These kids are the secret to selling cookies in large quantities! Let's leverage the genius of the Girl Scouts and bring your child in as your business' secret weapon for success!

How can your teen affect your business?

Soooo… are you ready to exploit your child? *<kidding>* But it is important that you emphasize what makes you special as a business. Being a part of a mother/daughter, mother/son, mentor/teen team is what makes you unique! Make sure you tell that story and celebrate it as often as you can in public. Use that to your benefit and make sure people know. There are four perfectly good reasons your child or teen is a boom for business, even if you don't take into consideration your teen's potential growth.

If you have a
TEEN
and you are running
your business like
EVERY other business
out there, you are
missing out on huge

Opportunity

and leaving money
on the table.

it's not always about
about
Changing
your **MIND**
but
CHANGING
your
Perspective

4 Reasons You Need Your Teen in Business

1. Higher Sales

We already established that no one can say "no" to a sweet little Girl Scout selling cookies, right?! Why do we support these little entrepreneurs? Is it because the cookies are amazing? Sure, but we could buy good cookies for a lot less at the grocery store. We support these girls because they are adorable. As women and as moms we are naturally nurturing. We want to support these children who are trying to better themselves. The same holds true for you in your business. How you incorporate your child is also important. We will give you some ideas for incorporating your teen in a later chapter.

NOTE: This is only applicable if your business is child-friendly. Do not include your child in businesses targeted at adult-only activities and products where it would be inappropriate. Including your child in an "adults only" business will not improve your business, but clearly do the opposite.

done properly

PARENTING

is a

Heroic

Act

-Edna Mode

2. Access

Your teen has access to people you don't; Teachers, coaches, activity leaders, dance instructors, Sunday school leaders, choir directors etc. These wonderful, influential people all see your teen on a regular basis. If you equip them to approach those people in a professional manner, these adults can open up new possibilities for your business. Team fundraisers, parties, a new customer circle are all a little outside your own reach, but directly within theirs.

3. Less Intimidating

People may not approach you in business because they find you intimidating. A well-spoken teen is often easier to approach and start a conversation. A warm, professional, teen greeting can be more welcoming to a potential customer. A successful experience with a teen in business can draw attention and bring additional income. The word will spread from woman to woman. As you know, we all talk to each other about our kids and everyone else's kids too. A good buzz will help your business grow faster than any amount of marketing or advertising.

4. Instantly Relatable

Having your teen join you in your business makes you instantly relatable. Why? Everyone out there has experience with a teen: they either are a parent, they had a parent, had a parental figure or at the very least they were a teen at some point in their life. That makes you instantly relatable to them through this common ground. They understand that your goal is to raise and train your child to be successful in life. Often they will be much more understanding of an imperfect sales routine than if you were making the sale alone.

Your teen can be your secret weapon in business. By including a polite, hard working, well-spoken teen in your daily business, you can find avenues to more success than you ever imagined.

PART 2
CREATING THE PLAN

CHAPTER 4

PLAYING IN THE SAME POND

If you're convinced that starting a business with your teen is the right step for your family, Congratulations! You have entered into one of the most amazing partnerships of your lives! That's right. You have taken the first step and significantly increased your chances of growing your teen. Now you must begin to shift your mindset and lay the foundation for your new business. Playing in the same pond with your teen requires setting up boundaries and rules of engagement before you get started. The more solid the foundation, the more likely you are to find success in your new endeavor. A strong house built on a weak foundation will not stand.

Spend time building the foundation well and you will set the stage for success and an unbreakable relationship with your teen.

The journey ahead will be more effective if you start with a major mindset shift. You are starting a business with a business partner. Begin thinking of your teen as your business partner. You may not be equal partners yet, but you are partners none-the-less. The sooner you can shift your thinking, the more quickly your teen will respond to being a business owner/entrepreneur.

As parents, it may be hard to make the shift— your child is your baby after all! You have nurtured and loved your son or daughter for years. You've tended to every need, kissed every boo-boo and protected your precious child from all the scary things that go bump in the night. It's hard to turn that concern, love, admiration, and adoration off. I'm not asking you not to love your teen. In fact, you will have to love your child a little more if that's possible. But for the sake of business, you will have to put aside your yearning to nurture and baby your teen if you hope to make this new training-ground work.

Consider your teen a new, responsible, young, co-worker or colleague. When your child becomes your business partner, he becomes your co-worker. If you were the manager at any other job and had a new employee to train, how would you view them? How would you treat them? How would you train them? Would you assume they knew anything? Would you use your sweetest voice and take things one step at a time? Would you be understanding when they fumbled? Would you talk down to them? If any other person came to work with you, what would they need to know about how you do business? Think through the things you need to do in your business. Don't make any assumptions about what your child knows. Start from the beginning and put yourself in training mode. Take the emotion out of your plans. Treat your teen as an inexperienced partner, not as your child.

Does this mean you have to look at your child as your business partner all the time? In business settings, yes you must treat your child as you would any colleague. Do I have to treat them that way all the time? Of course not! Mom and dad are the bosses at home! Enough said! You are still their parent and caregiver. Separating the two roles will not be easy, but setting boundaries will help delineate the two very different relationships you now have with your teen.

Communication

is **KEY** to

Success

with your **TEEN**

Lazy & the Nag

Samantha and I had some very loving names for each other in the first few months of business. We laugh about it now, but it was no joke back then. We called each other "Lazy" and the "Nag." Endearing right? Those who know us now often think we always had this strong, fun, playful relationship. People seem to think that God somehow showed favor on us, and *poof* we had this perfect relationship from the day she was born or something. Nothing could be further from the truth. Our relationship was ok when we started. We bickered and struggled to get along like most mothers and daughters. When we first started out as partners, we did not know how to work together. We hit every pothole in the road. We struggled through it and came out the other end stronger and closer, but it was a bumpy ride. Are you wondering where those sweet little nicknames came from? I'm confident you can guess. It certainly is not rocket science. In fact, many people have told us they could adopt the same nicknames for themselves.

Remember the party story? I thought she was being lazy because she was sitting in the corner reading while I worked the business. Well that was certainly not the only time I witnessed what I considered lazy behavior. I was so excited for this business that I couldn't wait to do all the things needed. Samantha didn't necessarily have the same daily excitement. I couldn't understand why she wouldn't jump right into the business as soon as she got home from school. Why would she not want to get started right away? Instead she would go watch TV or take a nap. I started reminding her often to get her tasks completed. She would push back and tell me she was tired and would do them later. Once again I thought she was being L-A-Z-Y!

It was happening so much that I setup a time for us to meet to talk about the business. I was prepared to discuss this very issue. I had wound myself up so tight, she was not going to know what hit her. I had all my points to make and she was going to see it my way. When I started our meeting, I delicately stated my case. Hahahahahaha. Who am I kidding?! I attacked her like swinging a sledgehammer of words against her head. Swing... and a MISS?!

What I wasn't expecting was that she was ready for me too. She had completed all her tasks on time. I didn't actually see her complete them, but she did. Then she proceeded to explain that she was tired of me reminding (aka nagging) her constantly about what needed to be done. She had the list and would get them done by the deadline, but she would not start working the minute she got home from school. She was tired after school and wanted to take a break. She went on to say that I needed to stop nagging her about the business all the time. These were well-developed, fair requests.

Wait! What just happened? I was out-maneuvered by a teenager. She was ready for the argument I had so carefully prepared. She completely disarmed me. I was speechless. As a mom I wanted her to do things my way and on my time. My daughter got tired of me nagging her all the time. The truth is I wasn't helping the situation. I was frustrating her and getting myself worked up.

We agreed that once tasks were assigned, I would not get involved or second-guess her anymore. We agreed I needed to back off a little and let her fail or succeed on her own. She was fully responsible. The good news is that she succeeded most of the time and typically had a good reason if she couldn't. You will find kids will succeed more than they fail if you believe in them and show it by allowing them to take the lead in those tasks.

She wasn't done with me though. She shot an arrow right through my heart with the next issue she wanted to address. She told me she "missed her mom." How could she miss her mom? She's spending more time with me than ever before.

As she continued to talk, I realized I had become business obsessed. As we began to find success with the business and with her development, I became more and more obsessed. Every time we were together I would talk about some aspect of the business. Every day, every meal, every ride home from school or drive to theater class was filled with business talk. When we sat and watched a movie I would bring it up. She loved the business as much as I did, but she wanted her mom back. She wanted and *needed* me to be her mom too and talk about typical mom things. I had lost sight of my number one job in life in lieu of this new role as her business partner. We had to find a balance to our business relationship and set some boundaries. The solution? The solution came in creation of weekly business meetings and a partnership agreement. We spent that meeting setting up some ground rules and our partnership agreement was born.

The next years were not perfect. What is? We argued occasionally and still do from time to time. But each time, we stuck to our ground rules and were able to work it out peacefully. We addressed each problem as it came up. We discussed issues without emotion as business women, but also with love and respect. We still do to this day.

The Business Meeting

The best way we've found to improve real business communication without impeding our mother/daughter relationship is to host a weekly business meeting. I recommend this route for you and your teen partner. Call it a business meeting. You are two partners meeting to discuss the status of your company regularly. Treat it professionally. The more you treat your business professionally, the more your teen will. They will take their cues from you and your attitude towards the business.

Your meeting doesn't have to be long, but you need dedicated time without the distraction of cellphones, doorbells, TV, friends, activities, laundry, other siblings etc. Show your teen that focus and commitment matter. Teach them what to expect in business meetings in the real world. Show your dedication to the business and give yourselves time to focus on the business, personal development and each other.

What to discuss?

What do you discuss in a business meeting with your teen? Put simply, you discuss anything and everything needed for you to effectively and efficiently run your business.

I've included a sample of our weekly agenda. It is only an example that worked for us. Use it as a starting place to create an agenda that fits you and your specific business needs. Be sure you print your agenda out as a guide each week so you and your teen stay organized and on track with your meeting.

Business Meeting

AGENDA

Forensics
(Discuss business from the past week)

review my notes on displays and taking orders

- What Should We Do Again?
- What Could We Do Better? ←

Think Tank
(Brainstorming Session)

Remember to pick up a whiteboard

- Ideas to Grow Business
- Ideas for Better Customer Service

New Business
(Discuss Coming Business and the Details)

- What's Coming this week?
- What's needed for Success this week?

Assignments
(Determine who will do each task)

- Assign Tasks
- Set Deadlines (date of completion)
- Update Calendar ← *post new calendar on office wall*

watch youtube speaker this week

Training
(Develop the WHOLE Person)

- Business Skills
- Personal Development

Agenda Item #1: Forensics

Talk about how the business is going. What did you do well in the last week? What can be improved? Use this time to address relationship struggles and partnership agreement infractions. Get everything out on the table with no emotion and no penalty for being honest. Remember, if you broke the partnership agreement, undermined or corrected your teen in front of a customer or client for example, you have to be willing to allow her to say so. Take a deep breath and take it as constructive criticism. As long as he or she is respectful in addressing the issue, you have to be open to hearing them out. The same holds true if they misquoted a price, sassed you in public or whatever your agreement stipulates. You both have the right to bring up any issues and address them as two professional business people. It's not personal. It's business.

The Golden Duck Parent Rule:

Leave personal issues outside the business meeting. If your child is getting a bad grade or didn't clean their room, this is not the time to discuss it. This time is set aside to discuss only business. You both need to know that this is a safe space. Don't muddy the water.

Conflict resolution is not easy for anyone. Add the parent/child dynamic, and you have a potential recipe for disaster. Walk slowly into these waters. If you can master this one thing, the rest of your tough issues will seem like nothing in comparison. You will not only be strengthening your relationship with each other, but teaching and modeling a critical life skill as well.

I encourage you to praise the positive. When something is done well, praise each other. Praise goes a long way to appreciating each other's efforts. We instituted a rule that really helped. For every negative feedback we gave each other, we had to have a positive too. Not only was that practice effective, but it kept us looking for positives in each other. Looking for the positive in people is another important life skill. You will be practicing two life skills on a weekly basis in this one step.

Possible Forensic Discussion Topics:

Setup, Signage, Displays, Handouts, Speaking, Greeting customers, Any business relationship notes, Sales, What's working? What isn't working? Did you have everything needed to complete your tasks? Should you do that event, party, customer's job again? Was it revenue generating? How much did you make last week? Etc.

Agenda Item #2: Think Tank

Discuss any new ideas. This is your time to get out a blank sheet of paper and let all your ideas fly. Write any idea down. Don't overthink them. Sometimes a seemingly silly suggestion can trigger another. Don't be quick to shoot down each other's ideas. Validate that they are good thoughts, but discuss the potential outcomes for each idea. Think of the pros and cons. Are there possible alternatives? Have you thought of any pitfalls?

This was Samantha's favorite agenda item. It gave her the outlet to showcase her creativity. Let your teen really throw out any idea they have. They have a very different perspective than you and often your teen's ideas will help you reach a different demographic. Even if an idea seems impossible initially, often it can be tweaked a little bit to work within your budget, time and restrictions or lead to a whole new idea entirely. We developed our own brainstorming formula for Think Tank time, we call it the BOP process.

If you get overwhelmed BOP it! Get your thoughts on paper, get organized and get your business back on track. Try the B.O.P. It process at home and in school too. It works.

Possible Think Tank Discussion Topics:

New Ideas, Brainstorming, How to expand the business, think outside the box.

BOP IT
BRAINSTORMING FORMULA

⇨ **BRAINSTORM**
⇨ **ORGANIZE**
⇨ **PRIORITIZE**

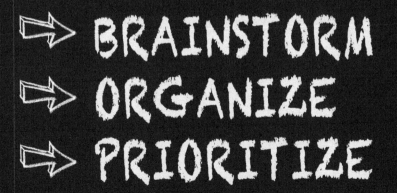

Brainstorming Made Easy

Give yourself a business boost with our B.O.P Process. Have you ever been overwhelmed with too many things to do in your business? Are you starting a new business and don't know where to start? In either case, brainstorming is a great way to catalog and organize your thoughts. We call our process the B.O.P. process or "BOP It" for short. Overwhelm can be overcome if you BOP it. It will work and can be done over and over to help you organize and prioritize the tasks in your business.

3 Easy Steps to Brainstorming and Overcoming Overwhelm in Business

BOP Step 1: Brain Dump

Start writing down every idea that comes to your mind. Fast... Don't think-- write. Write down every "to do," even words or incomplete thoughts should be scribbled down as they come to you. Do not try to organize these thoughts at this point. Write until you have nothing else left in your brain. You can also start a timer and do this in short increments weekly, or even daily, until you have a full task list.

BOP Step 2: Organize

Once you've completed your brain dump, read over the list. Add anything additional that comes to mind. Begin organizing. As you read through the list, you should start seeing some ideas and thoughts that go together or have a similar theme. Start putting similar ideas or topics together. For those that don't seem to fall into any specific topic, create a "Miscellaneous" or "Non-sense" category. Call it whatever makes sense to you. Read through the list until all items have been categorized into similar topics or categories. Look at the list again. Can you combine any similar categories? Simplify your list as much as you can now. It will make the next step easier. Continue working through your list until you feel confident you've got a good list of tasks under the fewest number of categories.

BOP Step 3: Prioritize

Now that you've organized your thoughts into categories, determine the order you want to address each category. Assign numbers to your categories. Consider these 3 questions when prioritizing.

1. *Which are revenue generating categories?*

Which categories are directly connected to bringing money into your business? Example: Cleaning or decorating your office may be important, but it will not generate any money for your business. Contacting former hostesses or clients will bring in additional revenue and should probably take precedence over cleaning your office.

2. *Which category is the most critical?*

3. *Which will yield the biggest return for your effort?*

Continue through all the categories. When all categories are numbered, do the same prioritization within each category. Once you are done numbering every category and item, set dates on your new priority list. Start with those given a number 1 priority, then number 2, number 3 and work you way through the entire list. By setting deadlines or goals, you are creating a sense of urgency. Goals will help keep you both progressing in your business. Priorities can and will change as you go, but this process will give you a good place to start.

Agenda Item #3: New Business

In the "New Business" section you will discuss what's coming up. Bring up new action items you need to plan for. You should update your calendar and discuss where you are in tasks assigned and when you expect to complete them.

Possible New Business Discussion Topics:

What's happening this week? What's coming up this month? What do we need to prepare for? Are we approaching any holidays? What tasks are needed to support the new business discussed? Do you need new supplies or inventory? Business cards? Update the calendar. Etc.

Agenda Item #4: Assignments

This item is critical for your sanity and success. I mentioned earlier in this chapter that my daughter endearingly named me, "the NAG!" While I don't want to admit it, it was true. We would assign tasks and I would expect her to complete her tasks when I wanted it--not necessarily by the determined deadline. I would remind her continuously. "Did you do x? Have you done Y yet? Don't forget you have to do Z before Friday!" All I was doing was annoying her and making myself crazy! How did we fix this? We agreed to adhere to assigned deadlines. She could get tasks done whenever she wanted as long as they were completed thoroughly by the deadline. I agreed not to remind her and had to let go.

I know what you are thinking. "What if my teen doesn't get it done by the deadline?" What if she doesn't get it done at all?" Did it happen to us? Yes it did. There were a couple of times she did not complete her tasks by the deadline. Any parent would think to herself, "If I'd stayed on her, she would have completed the task on time." While that may be true, what would that have taught her? Your teen would have learned that mom will always remind her what she needs to do, so there's no need to think about it, schedule it, or plan for it. If you jump in and do his tasks for him what does that teach? You teach him that mom will do his work for him, so why bother?

Actually, it's worse than that. Subliminally, your teen would be learning that his own parent doesn't believe he is capable. No parent would ever want to tell a child that, but it is exactly what kids think when parents jump in and do everything.

If your goal is to grow and develop your child, you must allow him or her to succeed or fail.

If your child succeeds he gets the rewards of a thriving business. If she fails, do not punish her. These tasks are not chores. If your child fails, withhold rewards. Your partner must learn there are consequences for actions (or inactions) in life. If your teen continues to fail, you need to have a discussion about the desire to continue in this business. Any employer would do the same. Remember, everything you do in your business is a teaching opportunity. Use these opportunities to your child's advantage.

Possible Assignments Discussion Topics:

Tasks, progress on tasks, check off tasks completed, assign new tasks, discuss better ways to accomplish tasks more efficiently, discuss and set deadlines for each new task.

Agenda Item #5: Training and Personal Development

The first step in working a business with your teen is to learn the business. That means you have to both dissect the business and teach it to your teen OR you have to learn the business together and help your teen master the specific aspects of the business you chose.

Bringing Your Teen into an Existing Business:

If you are bringing your teen into your existing business, you will have some homework to do upfront. Take some time and make a list of everything that needs to be accomplished to run your business. The easiest way to do this is to take a week in your life and write down everything you do. I mean everything. No task is too small. Every small piece makes up the whole of running your business. Counting inventory, placing stickers on catalogs, following up with customers, cleaning the workroom or buying supplies are all important tasks to a business. The mailroom to the boardroom is a journey your teen needs to learn. Don't take for granted that your teen will know these things need to be done or how to do them properly. Some may only take a few minutes to explain while others may take weeks or months to perfect. All are important.

Starting a new business with your Teen:

If you are starting this journey together from scratch, use this time to learn together. If you are starting a direct sales business, access training provided by your company. Search for helpful videos online that can help with how to run a business like yours. Talk to others who do what you do. People are usually willing to share their expertise with teens interested in pursuing their career. Use that to your benefit. Explain that you are starting this business as a way to help your teen develop and prepare for adulthood, to save money for college, whatever the ultimate goal. Even if college is not in your teen's current plan, people like to support kids that have a goal for the money they are making. Everyone was a teen once. They will identify with the struggle. If they don't, find someone who does.

Why do we need Personal Development?

Personal development covers activities that improve awareness and identity, develop talents and potential, build human capital and facilitate employability, enhance the quality of life and contribute to the realization of dreams and aspirations. Personal development takes place over the course of a person's entire life not only during adolescence. Yes, I could not say this more loudly or believe it more intently. Personal development is different than business training. While business training focuses on specific tasks and jobs related to running the business, personal development refers to the continuing growth of an individual throughout their life to better themselves as people and as leaders.

My favorite leadership expert and mentor, John C Maxwell, says this about growth: "Growth is the greatest separator between those who succeed and those who do not. When I see a person beginning to separate themselves from the pack, it's almost always due to personal growth." If you want to separate yourself from the pack, you must continue to grow. There is a big difference between 10 years of experience and repeating the same one year of experience nine times. Not only does this apply to your life, but to your developing teen's life too. Set your teen on a path that will help him stand out in the crowd. Teach her that we all need to continue growing.

How do I find Personal Development Topics?

The best thing about personal development is that there are many free online resources to help. This can be something that you do together. There is no reason that you can't choose topics that will grow both of you at the same time. Learning together is a great way to bond.

Every week you should plan one business training and one personal development. I will discuss intentional training in more depth in a later chapter, but be sure to leave time for both training and personal development even if it can't be on the same day due to time constraints.

MODEL
the *Character*
you want to
SEE
in your *teen*

The Partnership Agreement

Developing a partnership agreement needs to be the first topic of discussion at your first business meeting. You are going to set the ground rules for working together. Why? If you don't set boundaries up front, you will struggle with separating business from your personal relationship. Working with your teen is not easy, but neither is working with your parent. By taking some time to talk about ground rules and put them in writing, you will set yourselves up to avoid some of the biggest pitfalls of working together. Will having this piece of paper keep you from having disagreements, spats or frustration? No. But, it gives you a baseline to hold each other accountable to the promises and commitments you made when you entered this business relationship.

Where do I start?

Where do you start with a partnership agreement? The most important thing to know is that it does not have to be some legally formatted agreement. Remember, this is simply a set of ground rules for the two of you to follow. Honestly, this agreement can be handwritten on a piece of paper if that is what works for you. Don't let the term "partnership agreement" intimidate you.

Parent/Teen Partnership Agreement

I understand:
- ☐ That I am entering into a business
- ☐ That I will consider myself an entrepreneur
- ☐ That I am a responsible part of the success of this business

I agree that I will adhere to the following:

Relationship:
- ☐ Our relationship as parent/child comes first

Professionalism:
- ☐ I will be professional at all times when in a business setting
- ☐ I will not allow a bad mood or attitude to show around customers
- ☐ I will not Nag or Sass when it comes to this business
- ☐ I will not belittle or talk down to my partner
- ☐ If asked to do something in public, I will do it without attitude

Personal Issues:
- ☐ I will leave personal issues outside of our business
- ☐ There will be no talk about school or home life within business settings
- ☐ What happens outside business is personal and not to be repeated around customers or business colleagues

Time Commitments:
- ☐ I will attend EVERY weekly business meeting
- ☐ I will attend Training Sessions (even if they are at a different time)
- ☐ I will attend Personal Development Sessions with an open mind
- ☐ I will commit _____ hours a day/week/month to this business

Responsibilities:
- ☐ I will complete my work to the best of my ability by the deadline agreed upon
- ☐ Rewards/Payment will be given according to current agreements

Other: (Please write in anything specific to your relationship/partnership here):

_____

_____

_____

_____

Signed
_____
Adult/Mentor   Date
Signed
_____
Adult/Mentor   Date

What should the Agreement Include?

Below are a few examples from the partnership agreement Samantha and I created for ourselves. It is meant to be a guide. Talk through the points. Come up with your own. Write them down and sign your agreement. Both of you need to sign the agreement. Post it where you work or where you have your meetings. If anyone breaks the agreement without regard, the partnership is in jeopardy of being dissolved.

NOTE: This is a living agreement. As your relationship changes and your duckling matures you will want to re-address the agreement to better meet your changing needs.

Discuss the things that matter to each of you. What do you want from this agreement? How much do you expect from each other? How do you want to be treated? How many hours do you expect to dedicate to the business? Etc.

- Your Personal Relationship Comes First

  Whether you are a mother, father, aunt, uncle, grandparent or a friend of the family, your personal relationship comes first. Don't neglect that relationship for your business. Your teen needs their mom, dad, grandparent, and friend more than they need a business partner. Six months into our business my daughter told me she missed her mom and that she really needed her back. Her words hurt, but I was so proud that she was brave enough to say something. I took the criticism and we changed our agreement to reflect that my priority was to be her mom above anything else. Do yourself a favor and consider this point from the very beginning to avoid that mistake.

- Professionalism is expected at all times

Professionalism is so important in business. It is even more important to your teen if she hopes to be taken seriously as a business owner. No one expects a teen to be a business owner. They will overlook your teen as an authority until they see how you act towards them. People will watch how you interact with each other closely. They will look at how she treats you, but they will take their cues about your teen and their abilities from watching how you treat her. They will compare your relationship with their own parent/teen relationship or with how they related with their own parents. Show them a relationship to look up to. Be a role model as a pair. Be what others hope to be. In our agreement, we included items like "Don't nag or sass each other," "Don't correct each other in public," "Don't talk down to one another," and "If you are asked to do something, no matter if it's the adult or the teen asking, do it without attitude." Samantha knew I wouldn't correct her in front of anyone (remember, it's part of your business agreement). That commitment gave her the confidence to speak freely. If she made a mistake in tallying an order form, I wouldn't correct her until afterwards or at our next business meeting. Even then, I would tell her it wasn't a big deal, but that she needed to know to make corrections next time. In return she did the same for me. I let her make mistakes and stumble over her words. In the end it's ok if she didn't say things perfectly. If I'm honest, I didn't always get things right either, but we were in this together. We were a team and I needed to be her biggest fan.

The truth is that no one appreciates a combative relationship. It doesn't feel good being in one nor is it fun to watch. The more respect you show each other and your clients, the more comfortable you will make everyone around you feel. They will respect your relationship and view your teen as an entrepreneur. Mastering your business relationship with your teen will increase your customer's confidence in your business. Customer confidence means repeat business and word-of-mouth advertising. Don't miss those opportunities because of a bad day.

- Leave Personal Issues Outside the Business

We all have stuff. We have bad days. We make mistakes, have problems at school, arguments with friends and with each other. We deal with attitudes and bad moods. But to succeed you must leave them all outside the business. Discussing personal issues should be done in a family setting, not in your business meetings or around your business activities. Resist the urge to talk about personal problems with customers or around business functions. Much like you would not talk to your boss about your private life, you shouldn't talk about your private life to customers including your teen's life. It's a good habit to adopt.

- Time Commitments

  Determine how much time you will each dedicate to the business. If you only have an hour to commit to your business, be sure you set your goals accordingly. The more time you reserve for your business, the more progress you will make each week. Set expectations up front. Will you commit to X amount of hours a day? a week? a month? However you choose to set your minimum, declare it and put it in writing. This is a real business and requires time to develop. Your time commitments may not be the same. That's ok. But discuss them and how that will impact rewards and pay. Usually, more work means more pay. It's that simple.

- Schedule Weekly Business Meetings

  Be sure you are both committed to attending and investing effort in your weekly business meeting. Be present and engaged in the meeting. This is the cornerstone to running your business and will require full participation.

- Specify Terms that apply to your relationship

  Every partnership is different. Discuss items that affect your unique situation and be sure to add them to your agreement.

Define Clear Roles/Deadlines

By now, you should be thinking of your teen as a business partner. You understand you have a secret weapon for your business and you are starting to think about being intentional in teaching them what they will need to move towards adulthood. Now what?

Break down your business into small, bite-sized tasks. As your child masters one task, add a new one. Don't put your teen in the "do all the monotonous, menial tasks I don't want to do" role and leave them there. Would you want to do only that part of your business forever? Of course you wouldn't. You'd get bored and dissatisfied quickly. Your teen is no different. Your child can and should do those tedious things, but they are worth so much more to your business than those menial tasks alone.

We talked about those adorable Girl Scouts. Besides the yummy cookies, I love to see young girls trying to better themselves. I will support that all day long. Your teen is no different. Get your teen actively involved in your business, online social media, making customer calls, booking parties, etc. Your teen needs to be serving your customers, speaking to the crowd, telling his or her story, filling orders, training other teens, and so much more. All these things are based on the abilities of your teen, his age and what he can handle, but be sure to grow his roles as he grows or he will lose interest in the business.

How many times have we asked our teen to do something to turn around and do it ourselves? Late night projects they remembered the night before they are due? Lunches they forgot at home? Cleaning their room? The list is endless. I too, am guilty of it. The truth is that we are fixing the immediate problem, but creating a whole new one. By taking on their responsibilities we are setting them up for failure long term. We have to allow kids to succeed or fail while they are still under our protection. Those life lessons are critical to their development. The same holds true in business. If we define clear roles and expect them to complete their tasks we can avoid frustration and improve communication. Don't do their tasks or take over their role. They will surprise you at how much they can and will do.

"It's the struggles and lessons learned in **FAILURE** and hard work that teach our **TEENS** the skills they NEED *to Succeed* in life"

Communication is the key to succeeding in business with your teen. Map out clear responsibilities for each of you. Make sure tasks are appropriate for your teen's age and ability. Talk about tasks that need to be done. Be clear on exactly what is expected. Talk about new tasks. Train your teen how to complete each task assigned. Learn new tasks together. Use the combined learning experience as bonding time. Let your teen know she can ask questions if she is unsure how to complete a task. Be willing to adjust tasks weekly if you both feel it's appropriate. As your teen grows in the business, give her more responsibility. She has to be challenged to grow and to keep interest.

Agree to task assignments. Get your partner's input on the division of responsibility. Hold a weekly business meeting and make task assignments a regular item on the agenda. Make sure your teen has a list to refer to. I suggest your teen use a notebook, calendar or planner to write tasks down every week. The physical act of checking tasks off gives instant gratification and a sense of accomplishment. As your child becomes more comfortable in the business, ask your child to run the weekly meetings instead of you. Allow your partner to assign tasks to you as well.

Business Calendar

Introducing planners as a great organizational tool is optional but can be beneficial. Consider getting them an inexpensive planner for the business or print a simple calendar page on your computer for each month. Teens can add tasks and note deadlines in it. This is a tangible reminder of all the things expected of them. At the end of the week they can have the satisfaction of marking tasks off as they are completed. This may seem like a small thing, but little successes often make big differences.

4 STEPS

Step 1:

Family

Mark off all FAMILY activities first. These are non-negotiable dates that cannot be filled in with business.
Suggestions:
Sports activities
Music Lessons
Church
Family Dinners
Birthdays and Celebrations

Step 2:

Business Mtgs

Remember you are dedicated to your weekly Business meeting. Mark off those days/times.

Remember to include:
Training Times (if they need to be on a different day)

Personal Development Time (if they need to be on a different day)

Step 3:

Known Work/Events

The next step is to mark off all known work.

Include:
Jobs
Parties
Events
Fundraisers
Repeat Customer Work
Special Events
Marketing and Networking

Step 4:

Preferred Days

Don't leave the rest of your days empty. Mark days you PREFER to work. It's YOUR business, you choose when you want to work. Offer customers those dates first. Will you use an alternate date if needed? Of course! But, people like a couple of choices better than a blank/open calendar.

Miscellaneous Tips:

1. Front-Load - Fill your schedule starting at the beginning of your month first. By front loading your month, you can control and fill the back end as you work your month. This also helps you reach your goals more consistently/
2. Washi Tape - Washi Tape is an inexpensive, fun and EASY way to color code your calendar
3. Use what you have - You do NOT need a fancy planner. You can just print one on a piece of paper if needed. ANY calendar works. Use digital is that's what is most comfortable for both of you.

CALENDAR

MONTH						
SUN	**MON**	**TUES**	**WED**	**THURS**	**FRI**	**SAT**
	1	2	3 Business Mtg	4 VIP Customer	5 Open	6
7 Church & family	8	9 Open	10 Business Mtg	11 Fundraiser	12 Samantha's B-Day Celebration	13
14 Church & family	15 Open	16	17 Business Mtg	18	19 Business EVENT	20
21 Church & family	22 Open	23	24 Business Mtg	25 Open	26	27 Fundraiser
28 Church & family	29	30	31 Business Mtg			

5 Steps to Easy Calendaring

Once you have a calendar or planner, we suggest 5 easy steps to successful business and life planning.

Step 1: Family/Day Job

Mark off all family activities and any day job hours on the calendar first. These are non-negotiable dates and times that cannot be filled with business hours, tasks, events, jobs or parties, etc.

Include:

- Sports Practice and Games
- Music Lessons
- Church
- Family Dinners
- Birthdays and Celebrations
- Vacations
- Game Nights
- Movie Nights
- Date Nights
- Day Jobs
- Etc.

Remember family and personal time are critical to your quality of life and should be placed as your top priority when scheduling your time.

Step 2: Business Meetings

You are dedicated to your weekly business meetings. Mark off those days/times. If you show a dedication to taking your business seriously, your teen will also.

Include:

- Meeting Time
- Business Training Time (if on a different day)
- Personal Development Time (if on a different day)

Step 3: Known Work

Include:

- Jobs
- Hours of Operation
- Events
- Parties
- Fundraisers
- Repeat Customer Work

- Follow-up
- Special Events
- Setup and Break Down Time
- Marketing and Networking
- Etc

Step 4: Preferred Work Days (If applicable)

Don't leave the rest of your time empty. Mark days you *prefer* to work. It's your business, you choose when you want to work. Offer customers those dates first. Will you use an alternate date if it's needed? Of course you will. But, people like a couple of choices rather than a blank, open calendar.

Step 5: Miscellaneous Tips

- Front Load - Fill your schedule starting at the beginning of your month first. By front-loading your month, you can better control and fill the back end as you work through your month. This also helps you reach sales goals more consistently by jumpstarting each month with a lot of work.

- Washi Tape - Washi Tape is an inexpensive, fun and easy way to color-code your calendar. You can find it at any craft store, office supply and online. It is moveable. If a date changes in your calendar, it is easy to remove washi tape and reposition it on a new date. It's ok if you don't have washi tape. You can use colored markers or pencils to do the same thing.

- Use What You Have - You don't need an expensive planner. If you have one or want one, that's fine, but it's not necessary to plan well. You can print out a single month at a time from your computer. Any calendar will work. Digital calendars are also a great option that can be shared between you and your teen, but I highly recommend printing it out and keeping a copy to refer back to during business meetings. It is a great visual way to talk schedules without confusion.

LET THEM FAIL

You have to give your teen clear responsibilities and deadlines. If they don't complete a task, they lose the reward. Don't nag him. Don't do it *for* her. Don't remind your teen. Let her do it in her time. If she doesn't step up to the plate, she suffers the consequences—and so will the business. Why? Because you want to show your teen that you trust he will get the tasks done, and you need to give him the space to do it. Give him the chance to learn and show responsibility. Then, review how he did at your weekly business meetings. Absolutely insist that your child reviews you too. That's what good partners do.

Your teen can do so much more than you think. In your business, you have to be willing to delegate and allow your child fail. That's right... you have to let them fail. If you're teen doesn't fail often, you're not doing something right. Give her a responsibility and let her do it, even if it's not done the way you would do it or when. Let him try. Praise when he does well and coach when he doesn't. While working, don't go behind your teen and "fix" things to make it right. Keep a mental note of what you would have done differently and discuss it in your business meeting. Let your partner fail or succeed on his or her own. A small failure teaches much more than a big success.

A small failure teaches much more than a big success.

When your teen fails—and it will happen, sometimes miserably—what do you do? Do not punish. These are not chores! Take out the emotion. Business partners don't get punished. If they fail to do their share, they simply do not get to share in the rewards or compensation. There are consequences to actions in life. If you approach the working relationship with your teen with professionalism, instead of parent-ism, you will reduce the stress level for both of you. You will also allow your teen the opportunity to show you what he or she can do.

CHAPTER 5
THE FLIGHT PLAN

Samantha's growth didn't happen by accident nor did it happen overnight. It happened over months and years of intentional training and development. It came from creating and executing a very specific teen growth strategy. I call it our "flight plan." The plan was deliberate, even though it wasn't necessarily completely mapped out from day one. I continued to adapt and change the plan as time went by to allow for the growth I was witnessing in her. But I also added new topics as they came along too. I didn't think of all possible tasks or growth factors on the first day. My plan had to be flexible.

I will admit, I took lots of deep breaths when things didn't go perfectly. I had to allow mistakes to happen. That was hard for this perfectionist mom. I had to allow her to try things her way rather than always doing them mine. It took me stepping back and letting her take control slowly, as she was ready. Most of all, it took me swallowing my pride and looking for little wins for my teen rather than for myself. I had to create opportunities for her to find success. Short version? I had to chill out and make this time all about her. I needed to find successes for her and be able to celebrate her real success while taking a back seat.

> "You will not reach your goals by accident. Achieving what you want will take vision and intentional action over time."
> - Dave Ramsey

My plan had to have the ultimate goal of her becoming my replacement in the business. One task at a time, I needed to train her to do every piece of the business. I wanted to get to a point where she could do all the work herself.

If I could get her to take control and master every aspect of the business one task at a time, she would be ready to run it on her own when the time came. If she didn't want to continue with the business long-term, she would at least be armed with a vast skill set she could apply to whatever profession she chooses moving forward. I would essentially work myself out of a job and move her into it. I had to be ok with that. I was delighted when she stepped up to the plate with each new challenge. Thanks to her growth plan, I could track every step along the way.

Where do you begin? It's a big undertaking to prepare your teen to launch successfully into adulthood. The journey begins with intention. Be intentional in every task, goal, training and personal development. As the parent, mentor or leader you have to take a step back and consider this business as a tool. Some things your teen will learn simply by being around you, by watching you do them. But what about the things your child can't learn from watching you? Are you intentionally teaching those things? If you use this opportunity properly, your child can launch successfully and thrive from the very first step!

Being intentional implies you are doing something deliberately or on purpose. In this instance, you are creating a plan to teach your child everything that's needed to run your business and to succeed as an adult. We will call this your teen growth strategy. Let's talk about how to develop your own teen growth strategy.

There are two parts to developing your plan: Part One is called Business Training and Part Two focuses on Personal Development. Both parts are critical to the success of your child long term. *Get the Duck Out of My Pond: The Success Journal* is a great tool for your planning. It can help break all the pieces down to weekly tasks and allow you to track them for an entire year. While I really lobe our success journal, you do not have to have it accomplish the same thing. Find a blank notebook and devote it to training and personal development. Any notebook will work.

Achieving what you *want* will take

VISION

and

INTENTIONAL

ACTION

over *time*

-Dave Ramsey

Business Training

The first half of your plan, business training, may come more naturally for you. It is comprised of breaking down the day-to-day tasks needed to operate your business.

Get out a piece of paper. Yes, this is old school. You can obviously use a tablet, cellphone or computer if you are so inclined. To be honest, I am sometimes a little old school. I love the feeling of a fresh sheet of paper when I am brainstorming—it's a blank page with an undefined number of possibilities. Use what is most comfortable for you.

Make a list of all the key components of your business. This is truly a list. When you are done with listing everything you can think of, start adding some critical concepts for running a business in general. Use Google or Pinterest for ideas. You may have to learn or experience some of these tasks yourself before you can pass them along to your child. There is nothing wrong with that; in fact, I encourage it. This is a great opportunity to learn together.

You may not have a complete list from the start, and there may be some things that pop up or surprise you. That's perfectly fine. As new ideas come up, add them to your ongoing list. This is a living document. Let it evolve as you do.

Learn the Business Yourself

Once you have a list, you can start learning each task one at a time. If you are both new to starting a business, you can learn together. Be careful not to lose your teen's attention as you learn. Keep trainings short and interesting. What kinds of things should you train? Below are some suggestions, but remember to make the list your own and ask for input.

Training Topics to Improve Business Skills

- Filling out an order form
- Greeting customers and introducing yourself
- Writing emails and texts to customers
- Social Media for Business
- Packaging and mailing products (If applicable)
- Place stickers on catalogs (If applicable)
- Running credit cards or reviewing checks, or making change for cash-paying customers

- Creating fundraisers
- Finding new opportunities and potential customers
- Making Flyers and Presentations
- Thinking outside the box
- Creating graphics
- Sales tax
- Product knowledge
- Displays and merchandising
- Mentoring Others/Leadership
- Back office websites and systems (If applicable)

  Many companies have some type of Point of Sale system. Direct sales companies have back office systems. Learning them can be tricky.

- Tell your story (the "Why")

  Your teen's story is the key to endearing people to them and to your business. Their story is valuable! My daughter and I started every conversation, party, event or sale with Samantha telling her story. Her "why" helped her connect with women, it broke down barriers and made our potential customers want to support our business. She explained about being bullied and wanting to save money for college. Help your teen explain and naturally convey their "why" to an audience. Even if they are doing it to make some money to pay for extras like movies, a theme park pass, or clothing, tell that story. Practice, practice, practice!

- Creating Elevator Pitches

   An elevator pitch is a 60 to 90 second explanation of what you do. This is something that should be practiced out loud and timed. Often you only have a few seconds to tell someone about your business. Both you and your teen need to have this ready and memorized. You never know when an opportunity to tell someone about your business will come.

- Customer Service and Follow Up

   People appreciate companies that make them feel appreciated. Following up with customers after a purchase creates loyalty by letting them know you care. Thank you notes, follow-up messages, email and/or phone calls often solidify future business. Your teen can learn how to do these things, which is all part of regular business acumen. In addition it allows your customer another opportunity to purchase something they may have missed.

- Inventory

  Inventory is tedious, but so important. Learning to count inventory, how often to do it, and how to determine how much inventory to carry are great skills to teach your teen.

- Creating systems that can be duplicated

  Creating procedures for everything you do is critical to create consistency in the end product. It is also critical in the event you hire additional people to work with you. As you become more successful, you may want to consider hiring others to free up more of your time for important, moneymaking tasks. If you are in Direct Sales duplicity is critical to train people you sponsor and mentor to be able to follow your lead in the business.

- Incentives

  At the beginning of any business, the excitement keeps you motivated and inspired. When the newness wears off you may need to create fun incentives to help keep you both motivated. If you are part of a direct sales company, often this type of incentive is offered by your home office and easy to take advantage of. Trips, bonus cash, title promotions and product incentives are all common occurrences in direct sales and make great incentives to keep your momentum going. Setup your own incentives if you are not in a business that offers these things. By finding what you both like and attaching business goals to getting them, you can make incentives for yourselves. Always consider that the reward itself should equal the requirement to achieve it. For example, getting stickers put on a pile of catalogs probably wouldn't be enough to earn a trip to Disney, but selling $8,000 worth or product may warrant earning such a trip. Setting appropriate incentives and achieving them are both equally as important.

- Business Goal Setting

Setting goals is an important life skill. You can teach your teen how to set proper goals. There are many methods for setting goals. Samantha and I prefer the S.M.A.R.T. model, outlined below. Each goal should be SMART: Specific, Measurable, Attainable, Relevant and Timely.

You aren't going to learn everything in a week and neither will your teen. Remember the weekly business meetings? The last item on the agenda should always be training and personal development. Plan to spend at least 30 minutes or more weekly on Business Training, especially as you both learn the business. You can create a plan to focus on one business skill during each meeting until your teen has mastered them all. Review older topics on occasion to refresh skills that may need some improvement.

Smart

GOALS

S.M.A.R.T

Specific

(who, what, where, when, why, which?)

Does your goal answer these questions?

Know EXACTLY what you
want to accomplish and why

Measurable

(from and to?)

How will you measure your progress?

Make sure your goal can be
measured and tracked

Attainable

What are the steps you will take to reach your goal?

(how?)

Make your goal reachable
with reasonable effort

Relevent

(worthwhile?)

Celebrate when you reach a goal!!!

Your goal should be worth the
effort and meet your needs

Timely

← post your deadlines on your calendar

(when?)

Set a close deadline to achieve
your goal

Don't *tell* people your **DREAMS** *Show* them

Approach your

with

PROFESSIONALism

PARENTism

Finding Resources for Business Training

Where do you find all this training? Some training will be simple "show-n-tell." These show-n-tell trainings are always the easiest place to start. These are the hands-on tasks that are inherent to your business. After that, see if your company (if you go with direct sales) offers any live training or video modules you can use. If you are not part of a direct sales company use the internet to find additional training. Google is your new best friend. If you are part of a team, gather other leaders and break up responsibilities. Make training a group task. Delegate training to teammates, older teens, etc. It takes a tribe to raise a child. By delegating, you spread the responsibility and the workload with other parents and leaders. You can also give older teens the opportunity to teach too. This allows them the opportunity to learn leadership skills while teaching younger teens how to run the business. That's a win for everyone involved. Focus on the mindset of working yourself out of the business. Empowering your teen to train others is another big step towards their success and your departure.

Challenge: Take one week and write down everything you do in your business as you do it. Everything. Keep that list and add to it over time. These are the things you need to be sure your child can do. Your goal is to grow your child to the point where they can run a business all by herself or himself. If your teen chooses not to continue the business beyond his teen years, these skills will translate into any career or job they choose.

Personal Development

If you only focus on business tasks, you will teach your child to run a successful business. That is powerful. However, you will miss the opportunity to develop your child beyond business. You will have accomplished only half of the picture. If we want to make a real difference in the lives of our teens, we have to develop the whole person. That means we have to invest in personal development alongside our teens. Do you know that most kids today graduate high school and don't know how to write a check, balance their bank accounts, or change a tire? I realize few write checks anymore, but it is important to know how. Do you want your teen not to know basic skills? What kinds of things should you include in personal development of a teen? That depends on your teen, on your family and on your child's goals in the long term, but here are some basic personal development opportunities that are good for all teens.

Personal Development Topics to Develop the Whole Person

- Dressing for the proper occasion
- Greeting people and carrying a conversation
- Body language
- Car maintenance
- Cooking & Laundry
- Personal hygiene
- Banking & Budgeting
- Federal and State Taxes (Personal & Business)
- Manners
- Learning to take instruction and feedback
- Working with people/ interpersonal skills
- Financial planning and investing
- Saving money
- Credit cards, mortgages and car payments
- Writing a resume
- Applying to college and scholarships
- Philanthropy and volunteering
- Setting goals

Don't develop a little

Cultivate a future

BUSINESS
Rockstar

You are not developing a "little helper." You are developing a future business owner, executive, co-worker, CEO, parent, teacher, or even a future president of the United States. Personal development helps you focus on the many opportunities to enrich the whole person. This is where we lose most kids. If they don't have the skills and training to develop themselves, they will feel helpless and overwhelmed by the amount of work that needs to happen when they become adults. These are the things rarely taught in school or by parents today. Though it may seem hard to teach all these things, and you may get some pushback—keep going. Your teen will thank you for it in the future.

Finding Resources for Personal Development

Don't assume your child will know how to do things. No one knows everything, including parents. The good news is that you don't have to know it all, either. Personal development training is pretty easy to find. There are great resources online to help, including Google and YouTube. Search for personal development or a specific topic. Find child development experts and follow their Twitter, Facebook or Instagram accounts. Seek out local experts. Many will volunteer their time and talents to teach children. Use resources that are available to you and your child.

You should continue your own personal development also. Show them that adults don't know everything, and it's always good to continue to learn. Learning together can be a great bonding exercise. Let them know mom (or dad) is human, flawed and doesn't know it all. Show them that you are also willing to learn and improve as a person. Josh Shipp says "every kid is one caring adult away from being a success." You can be that one caring adult—for your kid or anyone else's.

"EVERY kid is one CARING adult away from being a SUCCESS." — Josh Shipp

---

Social Media for Teens in Business

The online landscape can be a frightening place for anyone, especially teens. Guiding your teen through the maze of trap doors can be scary. But there is so much opportunity online. In a world where your future is often determined by what people find about you on the Internet, it is important to talk to your teen about social media. Help your teen grow his influence and improve his online reputation. This topic is much bigger than this short overview, but below are five quick tips to get you thinking about online safety and your business.

5 Quick Tips to Start your Teen Online:

1. Privacy settings

Pay attention to the suggested privacy settings in the app. Most social media platforms (Facebook, Instagram, Snapchat, Twitter etc) have suggested settings for teens. Change settings to "friends only" or "private." This setting will not allow the general public to see anything your teen shares.

2. What you put online STAYS online

Teens need to know what they post (text or email) is permanent. Once it's online it can be copied and saved by others, even if your teen deletes it. Think twice about what you are sharing online, in text or in email. A good question to ask is, "Would you want what you are sharing to be placed on a billboard outside of school for all to see?" If the answer is no, don't send it! It's that easy.

WARNING:

Nudity Online: Every teen says they would never do it, but it happens way too often. If your teen receives or sends photos of nude teens, they can be prosecuted for child pornography. This is not a joke. Make sure your teen understands the ramifications of their actions.

3.   Never post your current location

We are constantly sharing every aspect of our lives. What we eat, who we are with and where we go are all common posts on most platforms. Sharing your current location online broadcasts where your teen can be found by anyone, especially bullies or potential predators. It's better not to post locations at all. But, if your teen wants to post photos of where she goes, suggest she post about it once she has left that location. Consider turning off GPS for most apps so these apps won't randomly be able to transmit where your teen is located without your teen realizing it.

4.   Tech breaks

This generation is brought up with screens in front of them, seemingly from birth. Most cannot remember a time without access to iPads, cellphones, TVs, laptops, etc. In fact, in America the average age a child gets their own tablet is 4.

This screen culture is hard to change. I don't think it needs "fixing," but we can adapt the culture enough to encourage occasional tech breaks. Time away from technology encourages social in-person interaction and conversation, exploring outdoors and more physical activity. Short tech breaks can change the focus of your teen to see a bigger world than the one inside the phone.

5. Don't text and drive

Did you know that texting and driving has now overtaken drunk driving in the number of fatalities amongst teens every year? Please emphasize that nothing is important enough that it can't wait a few minutes until your child gets to his destination. Nothing is so important that it is worth risking their life or the lives of others.

Public Speaking

Public speaking is one of the top three fears for adults, let alone teens. Your teen will be required to speak in front of class or another audience at some point. You can help improve their skills by giving them the opportunity to speak in front of small crowds often. In addition I've shared

5 quick tips to better public speaking. They are useful for both teens and adults.

5 Tips to Better Public Speaking

1. Practice

Much like an athlete has to practice their sport, public speaking takes practice. Plan your speech and practice it out loud over and over. Make notecards if needed to help you remember key points. Try using your cellphone to record yourself practicing. Watch it and be your own critic. Make adjustments and try it again. The more you practice this skill, the better you will be. Most people are not born to be public speakers. Even the most skilled speakers practice and hone their craft. Practice with your teen, even if you're a public speaking pro. One can never be too great of a speaker.

2. Slow down

Nerves always work against you. When people are nervous they tend to talk very fast. Think about your words. Consider a short pause to recollect your thoughts between sentences. Remember if you practice the way you want to present, you are much more likely to present the way you practiced. Practice at a slower pace than you usually speak because once you're in front of an audience, you will likely speed up your chat!

3. Make eye contact

Most people want to make a connection with a speaker. Don't look down at your feet. Find a few people in the audience and make eye contact. Speak right to them. It makes you relatable and believable. Don't speak ONLY to those people on the front row! Look around the room for the ones truly interested in what you're saying (not the ones scrolling on their phones!).

4. Don't fidget

Placement of your hands is very important. Fidgeting or wringing your hands shows the audience that you are nervous. Keep your hands still and calm except if you are making gestures for effect. Pointing, using your hands to list things or showing excitement through large movements are fine—it's the nervous fidgets you need to keep at bay.

5. Speak clearly

Speak as though someone in the back of the room is hard of hearing. Speak clearly and with enough volume that they entire audience can hear you. Don't mumble. You want to get your point across and make sure each person in the room can understand what you are saying. Recording your speech will help with this. Turn down the volume and listen without watching your video. Is your speech clear as a bell? If yes, hooray! If not, slow down and articulate each word. Repeat until clear.

Leadership

Teens often think you have to have a title or position to lead or be considered a leader. They also think they have to be an adult to be a leader. There is nothing further from the truth. In the book "Developing the Leader Within, 2.0," John Maxwell says: "Leaders become great not because of their power, but because of the ability to empower others." People want to follow leaders who care about them and who help them achieve their goals and dreams. A leader is someone willing to step up and work together to help those around them achieve their goals together. A leader has the mindset of "let's go do this together." Teens love doing things together with other people. Any teen can be a leader. Start helping your teen think like one. There is a wealth of information on leadership available in books, online or in social media groups. It's never to early to develop leadership skills, and these can make the biggest impact in the life of your teen.

the task

AHEAD

of you is

Never

stronger than the

STRENGTH

within you

PART 3
APPLYING THE PROCESS

CHAPTER 6
REWARDING THEM RIGHT

Keeping your teen's interest is critical. Believe it or not, your teen is not all that different from you in that aspect. We talked about the first step to keeping your child's interest by giving them increasing responsibilities over time. The second step is undoubtedly, rewarding teens for their efforts.

Why do you work? You work because it benefits you in some way. Whether it's working outside the home for a salary, working inside the home to benefit your household, or volunteering your time to benefit others, you do it because there is a benefit. When you work outside the home, you are rewarded for doing your job, right? You are paid for your efforts. Your teen is no different. I'm not saying you have to pay a big salary, but your teen needs to be rewarded according to the effort they put forth in the business.

Here's the thing, your child is not you! Your teen does not see things the same way you do nor do they have the same goals. Don't believe me? Take your teen shopping for clothes one afternoon. Their selections may curl your eyelashes, drive you to drink, or worse. Invariably, your teen would not choose the clothes you would, right? The point is that what drives you may not be what drives your teen. Find a reward system that works for your teen and stick to it. As your teen does more, reward more. It's that simple to keep an attention-seeking teen interested.

The reward does not always need to be money. Some choose to reward with other things—whatever motivates and inspires your child to keep going. Maybe start small, like going for ice cream, gaining screen time, or choosing a movie for family movie night. Younger teens particularly can be rewarded with earning time to do something they love. As your teen progresses in his efforts, move up the rewards scale to something like getting a manicure or pedicure together, shopping for something they've wanted for a while, or organizing a sleepover. Younger teens are often fine with rewards that are not monetary. All teens want your time, but if your teen is 15, 16 or 17, they will probably want cold, hard cash. You must discuss your rewards scale early in your business. It's never an easy topic, but money and rewards have to be clearly determined so there is no question what everyone gets for the labor contributed to the business.

Your teen must actually do the work required in order to earn the rewards. If they fail to complete tasks on time or to set expectations, they should not receive the rewards. Remember, business tasks are not chores. We don't punish for not completing a task. Give them a second chance to complete the work, if possible, and be willing to praise them when they do complete things well and by the deadline.

If the company you chose for your business offers incentives, and you truly work as a team to earn them, share those rewards with your teen. As a team, Samantha and I always knew we had to earn our incentive trips for two, and that she would be accompanying me on that trip. My husband did not love staying home, but he agreed that she did the work and earned the reward. Don't forget your teen when it comes time to receive these rewards. If you are considering direct sales, look around for one that offers teen programs. These businesses are out there and can help make this process a little easier.

What kind of things can you do to reward your teen partner? On the next page are some suggestions. Get your teen's perspective about how to be rewarded and agree to whatever the payment is in your business meetings. Revisit the topic as your teen's responsibilities grow.

a **GOAL** without a *plan* is just a *wish*

Teen Payment/Reward Ideas:

- Mani/Pedi
- Ice Cream or Favorite Dessert
- Special Dinner
- Bike rides, beach, pool time
- Game Night
- Movies
- Screen time
- Zip-Lining, go-carting, ATVs
- Paycheck (aka Cold Hard Cash)
- Percentage of the profit
- New cellphone or iPad
- Sleepovers
- Clothes Shopping
- Itunes or App credit
- Trips
- Share in company rewards
- Match their earnings (put money in a bank account for them so they can watch it grow!)

CHAPTER 7
A MATTER OF CHARACTER

Character is defined as being "the mental and moral qualities distinctive to an individual." Put differently, it is the true nature of a person. Abraham Lincoln said "Character is like a tree and reputation like a shadow. The shadow is what we think of it. The tree is the real thing."

A popular misconception is that character is something determined at birth. Jim Rohn said it this way "Character isn't something you were born with and can't change, like your fingerprints. It's something you weren't born with and must take responsibility for forming." Character is not part of your DNA. As much as we want to believe children are born with ingrained traits that guide them through life, character is actually developed and learned. Character is like a muscle. You must use it and practice it everyday to develop a strong moral compass.

> *"People of character do the right thing even if no one else does, not because they think it will change the world but because they refuse to be changed by the world."* - Michael Josephson

How do you develop character? You develop your own character by watching other people, by responding to events that happen in your life and by the choices you make on a daily basis. Character is influenced not only by intentional training, but by TV, movies, video games, social media, celebrities and friends. Every experience and emotion you have has played a role in developing your character.

Samantha went to a very large high school. She loved being one person in a very large crowd. She liked the fact that she could disappear. After her negative experience in a smaller school where she became the target of cruel bullies, she liked the anonymity. Anonymity was a blessing and she was grateful for every "invisible" moment.

In a school this large, lunchtime was always a madhouse. This school had one lunch period for over 3,000 students. There were groups of kids everywhere the eye could see for a full 90 minutes. They sat in classrooms, outside on benches, in the lunchroom, in the atrium, down every hallway and even on the floor by the lockers during lunch. Most brought their lunches because the cafeteria couldn't serve that many kids at one time. For a shy, self-conscious teen, this 90-minute break in the middle of the day with 3,000 other people was quite frankly, hell.

When Samantha finally found some friends, she was relieved and overjoyed. She was grateful to have someone to sit with and talk to. She would come home and tell me how amazing they were and how happy she was to have them. It seemed like we really had turned a corner. I was grateful that she was making connections and finding some social success of course, but I was even more grateful that the cruelty seemed to be behind us.

These kids didn't know anything about Samantha's past. They had no clue how much their kindness and friendship meant to her or to us. They treated her like anyone else and that was the best part. But, as the days and weeks progressed, things started to change. Then the day came when Samantha realized these "friends" were not true friends at all. She went to their lunch spot to find the group had moved to a new location and chosen not to inform her where or why they moved. She texted them but no response would come. No response to messages online either. Samantha found herself alone again. I don't know why these kids turned on her, but it didn't really matter. She was alone again in a crazy lunch madhouse with strangers. She couldn't leave or get away. Hurt and bewildered, she instantly found herself faced with the ugliness she thought she'd left behind.

This time, though, she had past experiences to draw from. She'd been through so much worse. She had a choice to make. She could choose to go back to being the victim of mean kids, or she could choose to stand up tall and move on. I'm happy to say Samantha chose to become a stronger, better person that day. She looked around and saw a girl sitting all alone in the corner of the atrium. The atrium was the largest space in the school. It was wide open and housed at least half of the student population at lunchtime. Much like herself, the girl was trying to make it through the next 90 minutes without incident. Samantha walked over and asked the girl if she could sit with her. The smile on the girl's face made my daughter realize the impact a small act of kindness could make. Did it change that girl's life to have someone to sit with? No. But, it did absolutely change the kind of day she was having. Sometimes all it takes is a small gesture to change the course of another person's day.

That day Samantha vowed to make it her goal to find one person each day that was sitting alone. She would ask to sit with them and make a new friend. She wasn't the only teen who was bullied, lonely or shy. Samantha was going to make a difference in the lives of others instead of feeling sorry for herself as a victim. She could make a difference one day at a time, one person at a time. She continued this habit through the rest of her high school career. She chose to form a good character trait of helping others. She made intentional decisions that helped form a character of kindness. She made lemonade out of lemons. She would tell you that choosing to be kind has blessed her even more than she blessed the recipients of her kindness. It's one of those amazing realizations in life that so few ever learn.

If character is a choice, what does that mean to you as a parent or teacher? It means that you have to be intentional in teaching character. Take advantage of every teaching moment when it happens to reinforce good character skills. Use weekly personal development time to talk about character. When you read a book, see a movie or hear a story, spend a minute highlighting both good and bad choices. Be present in the daily happenings so you can guide your teen to make the best choices in developing good character.

Commitment

> *"Commitment is doing what you said you'd do long after the mood you said it in has left you."* -Darren Hardy

When you tell someone you will do something, you need to follow through every time, whether you want to or not. Commit to following through, regardless of the person you made the commitment to, the kind of day you are having or the better offer you get. People have to know they can depend on you.

You can't tiptoe into success. You have to own it. You have to be committed to doing everything it takes to reach your goal. You have to be all-in. Be willing to dig deep and do the things needed even when you don't feel like it. That's how people reach their dreams, one day at a time. Take small steps and do one task at a time to reach true success.

COMMITMENT
is doing what you

Said

you'd do
LONG after
the **MOOD** you
said it in is

Gone
-Darren Hardy

As parents we can encourage our children to commit and follow through. We can help them make tough decisions when activities are in conflict. Help your teen decide which commitment to make and show them how to stick to those decisions. In theory this sounds easy, but teens will often struggle when a better opportunity presents itself. But once your child has made a commitment, you must help teach them to follow through even if it means they miss out on something that sounded more fun. In the long run, your teen will benefit from showing that they follow through every time, no matter what. What your child will gain is the respect and trust of those around them—and the ultimate success that comes with that.

Forgiveness

Forgiveness is tough. When people hurt you or someone you love, feelings of anger often take over. Those feelings are strong and can consume you. They can become so all-encompassing that they take over every thought and action. By feeding these feelings and allowing the hate to fester inside, you allow yourself to continue being the victim. To break free of such strong feelings, you have to learn to forgive and let go. Forgiveness is not for the person being forgiven.

It is for you to find peace and regain control of your life.

When I began hearing the flood of stories about what Samantha had gone through at the hands of her bullies, I was angry. Correction. I was angry and downright pissed off! I wanted those kids to hurt every bit as much as my daughter had been hurt. I wanted them to suffer the long-term affects of bullying like we had been suffering with Samantha. I wanted them to be marked with a giant letter A like in the book The Scarlet Letter. I wanted everyone to know what these bullies had done. I wanted them to be ostracized like they had done with my child. God forgive me, but that's exactly how I felt.

It took a long time for me to realize that my hate was fueled not only by anger but also by guilt. I felt an incredible sense of guilt for not being able to be there for my daughter and for missing all the signs that were screaming to be seen. I was her mother. It was my job to protect her. All the signs were there and I had fallen asleep at the wheel. It took years of prayer, self-evaluation and seasons of binge watching "The Sons of Anarchy" to come to the realization that hurt children learn to hurt. There is nothing like a seriously dysfunctional, outlaw biker gang to make you feel better about your situation.

Seriously! But children learn to hurt by being hurt themselves. Those kids who hurt my child likely were dealing with their own deep-seeded pain. The need to hurt an innocent young girl because she was heavy, because she was different, had to be born from a hurt so egregious that is spilled out onto others around them. Samantha was the unfortunate target for their release, but she had a loving family and a strong faith for support. I eventually forgave those kids for hurting Samantha. I had to forgive them to find peace for myself and for my family. The more I clung to the hate, the more it hurt us all. The more it hurt Samantha. I had to let it go.

Teach your teen the importance of forgiveness over the need for vengeance. Help your child develop love for others and a love for themselves that is strong enough to overcome anger and despair. "Forgiveness is a trait of the strong" Matatma Ghandi said. The world needs so much more of it.

Especially in business, the need for forgiveness is real. Forgive the person who shuts the door in your face. Forgive the person who cheats or lies to you about your products or business. Forgive the person you thought you could rely on but who never showed up. Forgive the person who spreads negativity about what you're doing.

Acknowledge these things are their problem and forgive them for bringing it to you. Only then will your business continue to soar!

The MOST important
thing you can do
for your

TEEN

is to continue

your own

development

Willingness to Learn

Everyone has an opinion. It is absolutely ok to have one. If you don't have an opinion you aren't thinking for yourself. But, we have to have a spirit of being open-minded. The more we can learn about everything around us, the more we can understand those who don't agree with us. We should crave knowledge about everything and anything. If you can teach your teen to love learning and be willing to learn, they will continue to grow and evolve through the rest of their lives.

How do you foster a willingness to learn? You do that by encouraging your teen to find out more about things that interest them. Some teens don't like school. Those are the kids that will need to find things outside of the classroom that keep their interest. Find the fun in learning. Let them know that learning doesn't always have to be boring or hard, and it doesn't have to come from a textbook or a classroom. By encouraging them to learn for enjoyment, they will find enjoyment in a pursuit of knowledge that will extend far beyond their school years.

Courage

What is courage? It's a hard thing to define. Courage is an inner strength that empowers people to take difficult circumstances head on. It is not the absence of fear. It is the ability to act in the face of fear. It is the concept behind the saying, "Do it scared." It's ok to feel fear. We all have moments of fear. It's our body's natural reaction to things that scare us. It's a natural defense mechanism that alerts us that there is danger. But those moments of fear where you can push forward and act anyway are the moments you show true courage.

Share with your teen when you are scared of something. Let them know that everyone faces fear, even adults who may seem so brave. Show him that we all have times we have to do something scared and we all live to tell about it.

When your child is scared, assure them it's okay. Reassure them that no matter the outcome, they are a winner for pushing through and completing the task. Let them know that half the battle is having the courage to show up.

Loyalty

Loyalty is faithfulness to a person or an obligation. Loyalty is a key pillar to good character. Being loyal to the people who mean the most to you means sticking with it when times are hard every bit as much as when times are easy. I found an amazing quote to think on when you consider the character trait of loyalty. "Those who don't know the value of loyalty can never appreciate the cost of betrayal." - Unknown. The best way to teach loyalty is to show loyalty. Show loyalty in your family and in your friendships. Do your teens hear you talk positively about others? Do they see you jump to help another person when there is a need? Or do they see you drop people at the first sign of discord? Loyalty breeds loyalty, remember that.

You have
ONE LIFE
set
Bigger
GOALS

Self-Discipline

Self-discipline goes hand-in-hand with commitment. Once you've made a commitment to do something, self-discipline is the ability to control your actions and follow through with that commitment. It's doing the things needed every single day to complete your tasks and better yourself. Self-discipline is different than discipline. Discipline assumes there is a third party correcting your actions and motivating you to do better. When you can regulate yourself to do those things, that is self-discipline. You can be your own motivation. Self-discipline is the one thing necessary to achieve any goal worth setting.

Samantha was bullied because she was a heavy girl. Food became her only friend and her weight skyrocketed. She had said she wanted to lose weight, but she lacked the self-discipline to avoid the foods that she loved. In fact we all were junk food junkies. Knowing she was unhealthy, she feared moving forward in her life at her size. Weight affected every aspect of her day. She had to consider her weight whenever she wanted to do anything. She had to think things like: Did she need a seat extender on an airplane? Could she fit in a chair offered to her? Could she walk as far as she needed to get to class? It was enveloping her life as much as bullying had. She had found confidence and love for herself, but she still lacked the self-discipline to focus on her health. In 2017, she made a commitment to focus on getting healthy. A year later, she had lost over 100 pounds. But her journey is not over. Now she has to keep it off. She will have to continue to make good choices for the rest of her life. She has to show self-discipline every single day to exercise, eat the right foods and avoid the foods she knows are not good for her. No longer does her weight define her. She is healthier than ever, but more importantly she has learned that through self-discipline she can achieve anything she wants in life.

She started learning self-discipline through our business. She had to do the tasks for each goal she set. The drive to achieve the rewards that came from reaching each goal had to come from within her. While I held her accountable, I did not discipline her when she didn't complete the tasks. Eventually, your teen will learn how to be self-disciplined if you allow them to complete tasks, make mistakes, FAIL and push forward to reap the rewards.

Gratitude

We spend way too much time wanting *stuff.* We often seem insatiable in our yearning for more and more. Gratitude is a habit. Intentionally reminding ourselves how much we already have will help quench that need for more. Appreciating what we already have and what people do for us causes some amazing shifts in our lives. We start focusing on others rather than ourselves. When we have a habit of gratitude we improve our health and emotional wellbeing. It is this constant abundance mindset that can be the difference between finding true happiness and never being satisfied. It's a choice. Choose to be grateful for what you have.

Gratitude is the easiest character to model. Parents often forget to thank their teens for the things they do. A simple "thank you" when your teen picks up his backpack or loads the dishwasher can go a long way. Show him that you are grateful for things people do for you. Have her write thank you notes. Encourage him to say thank you when someone compliments him or holds a door for him. Encourage them to keep a gratitude journal everyday. Start your business meetings with something you are each grateful for. These are easy daily reminders to be thankful for what we have in this moment.

Responsibility

Taking responsibility means taking ownership of your actions. Deciding to set high standards, learning from our mistakes and following through on our promises all make for responsible character. It's the attitude of "no excuses" that makes the difference between the strong and the weak. We need to teach our teens to be accountable to themselves for their actions and commitments. Have your teen ask themself questions like, "Do I do what needs to be done?" "Do I follow through on my promises?" "Do I think through the consequences of my actions?" "Do I blame others or accept those consequences?" "Am I reliable and dependable?" The answers to all these questions are the key to developing a sense of personal responsibility. You may want to ask these questions of yourself, too. Accept responsibility for your life. Know that it is *you* who will get you where you want to go.

Trust

There is not much to say about trust except to give a warning. Trust is not given. It is earned. It takes a long time to earn someone's trust. Trust is developed over weeks, months and years of continuous opportunity to show that you are trustworthy. On the flipside, it can take mere seconds to lose someone's trust. The slip of a tongue or a bad choice of action, and—poof! That trust is broken. Consider this truth every single day. Make choices that will make you trustworthy. Trust is like a piece of paper. Once it's crumpled up it can never be the same. Talk about this topic, and about building or breaking trust in your business meetings or even after a business event. Help your child point out instances when trust was built or broken.

Independence

Have you ever met a two-year-old who didn't want to do something themself? "I do... I do" and "Me! Me!" is what we heard when our kids were toddlers, over and over again. Kids naturally want to do things for themselves. There is a sense of pride that comes from standing on your own two feet and doing as much as possible for yourself. A teen that shows a desire for independence learns responsibility.

Foster a sense of independence in your teen by not doing everything for them. If they forget to do something important, they will surely remember the next time. Encourage them to complete projects on their own. If the projects are difficult, help them break it up into attainable steps they can take on their own. Resist the urge to fix all your child's mistakes. Let them stay up all night completing a project. Help them if they get stuck of course, but let them do the work and allow them to fail if they don't. If they forget their lunch, don't bring it to school for them. They will survive one day without a lunch if there are no medical issues to consider, I promise. But, chances are, they won't forget their lunch again if it means that much to them. Teens will learn much more from a small failure than they will ever gain from a big success.

Teens will learn much more from a small failure than they will ever gain from a big success.

Initiative

Taking initiative does not mean being pushy, obnoxious or aggressive, but recognizing your ability to make things happen. Initiative is an inner motivation that drives you to do things others will not. Encourage your teen to be the first to start something new or help a teacher who has their hands full. Let your teen know that doing something that needs to be done without having to be asked is far better than waiting to be told. But also let your teen know not to do things for praise or accolades, but in an effort to serve others. Taking initiative is rewarding and character-building. In your business meetings, ask your teen partner what initiative they can take during the week and watch your child's development take off!

Perseverance

No ones likes failure or difficulty. Teach your teen to push through and meet challenges with determination. Life will not always be easy. Parents who remove all obstacles from their child's life, won't give their offspring the tools needed to succeed when life doesn't go as planned. Allow your child to face little struggles while still under your care and protection. Your child will learn to get back up and keep trying. Don't let the first failure your teen faces come as a young adult. The consequences could be life altering. Those who never give up will find success no matter what.

> "Many of life's failures are people who did not realize how close they were to success when they gave up." -Thomas A Edison

Honesty and Integrity

No one likes a liar! A liar can't be trusted, isn't well liked and typically is not included. Honesty is easy until there are consequences for the truth. Telling the truth when it is difficult not only builds personal character, it shows integrity. In our house, we always rewarded honesty with a lighter "sentence" so-to-speak. Our kids knew that being honest was always the best choice. They knew if we found out they had not told the truth, their punishment would be doubled. Let your teen know how important honesty is from the very beginning. Be sure you let them know that lies of omission are still lies. It is said that "integrity is choosing your thoughts and actions based on values rather than personal gain."

"Integrity is choosing your thoughts and actions based on values rather than personal gain"
- Unknown

Kindness

We call it being a "Force for Good." Kindness is the act of true charity. Thinking of others more than yourself and helping where you can is the basis of community. Strong leaders are sensitive and kind. They learn to look at situations from another's point of view and modify their words or actions appropriately. This skill will earn your teen loyalty and respect from their peers.

I will never forget the first community egg hunt we attended when my son was in kindergarten. He returned with no eggs in his basket, but a smile on his face. I knew he had found a lot of eggs. Where had they gone? He proceeded to explain that he had given all his eggs to a two-year-old little girl who didn't find any eggs herself. When I asked him why he gave her all of them, he simply said "because it made her happy." Most kindergarteners know instinctively to be kind. If we continue to foster kindness instead of getting everything feel we are "owed" or "entitled to," our kids can grow into kind teens and adults.

> *"No act of kindness, no matter how small, is ever wasted."* -Aesop

A kind word or a simple "hello" can make a huge difference in someone's day, yet is takes only seconds. We all want to be liked, have friends and feel accepted. There is an inherent need to be a part of something and have a sense of community. Acknowledge the cashier at the market. Help an elderly woman carry a package to her door. All people are valuable and deserve respect. Real leaders put down their cellphones and "see" the people around them.

We lose the sense of human connection thanks to cellphones and computer screens. As a society, we have distanced ourselves from each other by communicating only through the safety of a screen. People will text, post and message things through a screen that they would never say to someone in person. Why? There are no visible reactions when you communicate through a screen. We don't see the anger, feel the sadness or embarrassment, or hear the inflection of the human voice. We've become numb to other's feelings because we don't see the reaction. We are empowered to say whatever comes to mind. We've become a society of mean girls (and boys). Your teen can change that by showing respect online and in person.

Saying "thank you" and "please" is a great way to start. Teens who master the art of being polite are typically seen in a much more positive light than their peers. When a CEO or politician gets up to speak, the first thing he or she says is "thank you" for the audience's time and effort. They do this first because leaders know the value of showing others respect, politeness and courtesy. Politeness is the most important of all common courtesies and the most underestimated. Practice scenarios for when your teen can be polite to others. Don't assume your child will inherently know this. Make it a point to model and discuss this critical trait in your weekly meetings.

Model the character you want to see

Teaching character is only part of the equation. Children will model what they see in you. As parents and teachers we need to set the standard by showing the character we want our teens to develop every single day.

If someone cuts you off in traffic what do you do? Do you scream, curse and flip-off the driver? Or do you let the other driver pass and say something like, "Obviously he needs to get somewhere faster than I do." It's not always easy to make the right choice in the heat of the moment, but it is critical to your teen's development.

You are responsible for the choices you make to build your own character. How you act and how you treat others are all choices. You have the power to change a bad choice to a good one. You can turn a bad day into the best day. See the potential in the positive. The choice is truly yours. You can't control what happens, but you can control how you react. By making positive choices, you build a character that will catapult you to the best life you can have. Be sure you are showing your best self to your children everyday in everything you do.

> *"You are free to choose, but you are not free from the consequence of your choice"* - Unknown

It's all about choices. There is no greater responsibility than to take on the development of the next generation. If we want to make a difference, prepare our youth with the skills to make good choices and develop great character, we must begin with making our own choices intentionally.

KINDNESS
is a gift

Everyone

can afford

CHAPTER 8
MAKE A DIFFERENCE

Teens and business may seem like an odd combination. Many think working with their teen will be too frustrating to be worthwhile. The truth is if you have a teen and you are NOT including them in your business, you are leaving huge opportunity on the table. You can actually grow your bottom line, your teen and your relationship all at the same time.

By partnering with my child I was able to watch her go from a bullied, shy, self-conscious teen to a thriving, young adult. Together we exploded our business, became one of the top producing teams in the company, grew an international team, earned company incentive trips, a company culture award and paid for Samantha's college tuition in the process. Where is she now? Samantha is a thriving college student. She's on the dean's list, active in her sorority, a leader on campus and volunteers her time to many charities weekly. Every day she has a goal to put a smile on the faces of at least 5 random people. She has made it her passion to teach others what she's learned through her journey. She's learned that you can't let what others think about you define who you are because they don't know you. She learned that there is life after bullying. She's learned that she is good enough the way she is. We often get the opportunity to speak and train parents and teens together and it's become our joint passion.

I tell you all of that not boast or brag, but to encourage you. What we were able to accomplish is not magic nor is it rocket science. With an intentional strategy, patience and a lot of love you can affect the future of your teen too. Build a relationship you never imagined possible. Guide your teen to develop strong business skills and a strong character that will stay with them long after they have launched into adulthood. Are you willing to make the difference in the life of a child? Their future depends on it, but so does yours. The best part of our journey I can only tell you in Samantha's words. These words made the journey worth every effort.

> *"My whole life people have always said I am not skinny enough, pretty enough or good enough. But, I know now that I am enough the way I am... the way God made me."*
> -Samantha Brantley

"A hundred years from now it will not matter what kind of car I drove, what kind of house I lived in, how much money I had in the bank... but the world may be a better place because I made a difference in the life of a child." -Forest Witcraft

---

My whole life people
said I wasn't
GOOD ENOUGH
Pretty enough or
Skinny enough.
I know now that

Just the way I am

- Samantha Brantley

If your **TEEN** doesn't **FAIL** *Often,* you're doing *Something* **WRONG**

ACKNOWLEDGMENTS

I want to acknowledge my faith publicly. I'm grateful every minute of my life for my savior Jesus Christ who carries and guides me every single day. He is my anchor and provides my moral compass in all I do.

I want to say **"Thank you"** from the bottom of my heart to:

My amazing husband, **Sean**, who is my best friend, biggest cheerleader and source of strength. Thank you for loving me unconditionally, for knowing the right thing to say and when to say nothing at all. I love you baby!

My daughter, **Samantha**, who inspires me to not only be a better mom, but a better person. Thank you for reaching for the stars and pushing me to do the same.

My son, **Doug**, who challenges me to think outside the box and look at things in a different way. Thank you for having such a beautiful, giving spirit.

My parents, **Bob and Hope Weiss**, who raised me as they live their lives, with great love and integrity.

My tribe who are all smart, strong, amazing women. To me, they will always be **LEGENDS**. Thank you for reminding me to stay in my own lane.

My editor, **Ana Prokos**, who has become a valued, lifelong friend. I could not have made it through this process without you!

The "**Duck Pond**" community for doing life together. Life is so much better when you don't have to do it alone.

RECOMMENDED RESOURCES

Books & Audio

- **Get The Duck Out of My Pond: The Success Journal,** Sandy Brantley
- **Growing Up Social,** Gary Chapman and Arlene Pellicane
- **The 5 Love Languages of Teenagers,** Gary Chapman
- **Success for Teens,** Editors of the Success Foundation
- **Raising Teens in a Contrary Culture,** Mark Gregston
- **Tough Guys and Drama Queens Parent's Guide,** Mark Gregston
- **Screens and Teens,** Kathy Koch
- **Daring and Disruptive,** Lisa Messenger
- **Sometimes You Win Sometimes You Learn for Teens,** John C. Maxwell
- **The Teens Guide to Social Media and Mobile Devices,** Jonathan McKee
- **Notes to a Young Entrepreneur,** Gary Nealon
- **Teen Entrepreneur Toolbox,** Anthony ONeal

- **Smart Money Smart Kids**, Dave Ramsey and Rachel Cruz
- **No More Perfect Moms**, Jill Savage
- **Become a Teen Boss**, Kevin Speights
- **Micro Business for Teens Workbook**, Carol Topp

Organizations, Websites & Social Media

- **The Duck Wrangler (aka Sandy's Website)** TheDuckWrangler.com
- Admission Smarts admissionsmarts.com
- BossMoms facebook.com/groups/BossMomGroup
- Heartlight; Parenting Today's Teens heartlightministries.org
- Grown & Flown facebook.com/grownandflown
- Parent Engagement Network parentengagementnetwork.org
- The Success Foundation SuccessFoundation.org
- Teenpreneur Inc Teenpreneurinc.org

ABOUT THE AUTHOR

Teen growth evangelist Sandy Brantley is a former fortune 50 executive, speaker, trainer, coach, wife and mom of 2. Known as "The Duck Wrangler," she consults with individuals and companies across the U.S. in leadership and developing teens using good business practices and strategies. Her goal is to foster a more employable generation of young adults. After witnessing the cruel affects of bullying on her teen daughter, she started a journey that has changed both of their lives forever.

Sandy has had a somewhat eclectic career including being an on-air guest host for HSN and owning a successful curriculum development company. Never interested in direct sales, Sandy decided to join a social selling company at the plea of her then 16-year-old daughter Samantha. Seeing it as a way to help Samantha heal, find success and gain confidence, Sandy jumped in with both feet. Within a year, they became top producers in their company, built an international team, and put money away for college. Sandy used her knowledge in business and leadership coupled with lessons she learned during their journey to create an easy to follow growth strategy. This strategy helped transform Samantha from a shy, self-conscious teen into a confident, thriving young adult. Sandy now shares what she's learned in her quest to empower parents, teachers, child professionals and businesses to better prepare their own teens to launch successfully.

Your Next Steps with
THE DUCK WRANGLER

GRAB A COPY OF THE SUCCESS JOURNAL

- Create daily success habits
- Open lines of communication
- Track meeting agendas & tasks
- Develop a business training plan
- Focus on modeling good character
- Document weekly goals & progress

FINALIZE THE AGREEMENT
Download our FREE parent-teen agreement
theDuckWrangler.com/contract

JOIN THE DUCK POND COMMUNITY
Come do Life with us...  #theduckwrangler

DISCOVER OUR ONLINE COURSES
Dive Deeper & Start Parenting with Intention

find out more
theduckwrangler.com

JOIN US ON **facebook**.

THE DUCK POND
a community commited to launching our teens successfully

THE DUCK WRANGLER

...come do LIFE with us
#theduckwrangler

Level up in ALL aspects of your LIFE
No matter where you are looking to improve your leadership

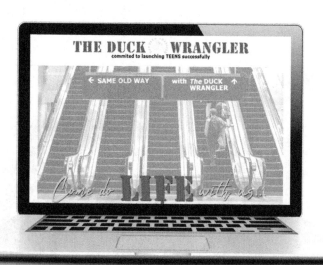

For more resources and to follow my blog

theduckwrangler.com

Made in the USA
Columbia, SC
20 May 2022

60682663R00098